REINVENTION

Sewing with Rescued Materials

Maya Donenfeld

John Wiley & Sons, Inc.

Senior Editor
Roxane Cerda

Project Editor
Charlotte Kughen, The Wordsmithery LLC

Editorial Manager
Christina Stambaugh

Vice President and Publisher
Cindy Kitchel

Vice President and Executive Publisher
Kathy Nebenhaus

Interior Design
Jennifer Mayberry

Cover Design
Wendy Mount

Photography
Deborah Donenfeld

Published by John Wiley & Sons, Inc., Hoboken, New Jersey

Published simultaneously in Canada

For general information on our other products and services or to obtain technical support please contact our Customer Care Department within the U.S. at (877) 762-2974, outside the U.S. at (317) 572-3993 or fax (317) 572-4002.

Wiley also publishes its books in a variety of electronic formats and by print-on-demand. Not all content that is available in standard print versions of this book may appear or be packaged in all book formats. If you have purchased a version of this book that did not include media that is referenced by or accompanies a standard print version, you may request this media by visiting `http://booksupport.wiley.com`. For more information about Wiley products, visit us `www.wiley.com`.

Library of Congress Control Number: 2011945556

ISBN: 978-1-118-07753-5 (pbk)

ISBN: 978-1-118-22270-6 (ebk)

Printed in China

10 9 8 7 6 5 4 3 2 1

Book production by John Wiley & Sons, Inc. Composition Services

This book is dedicated to my grandparents, Tom and Beverly Howe, the wisest and most resourceful people I've ever known.
They taught me to trust my heart, use my head, and work with my hands.
It was written for my grandchildren and yours, for they will be the ones to reinvent what we don't rescue today.

Acknowledgments

I could never have created *Reinvention* without the contributions of so many fantastic people. First and foremost, I would like to thank my online community, which includes the most loving and creative readers ever! I am deeply grateful to:

Linda Roghaar, my wise and gentle agent, who guided me with compassion and sensitivity.

The creative and dedicated team at Wiley who embraced each step of the way with enthusiasm. Huge thanks to Cindy Kitchel, Roxane Cerda, and Charlotte Kughen.

All of the project testers for their valuable input: Elizabeth Rea, Lindsay Conner, Angela Condon, Tammy Mattox, Denise Muller, Jenny Shroyer, Veronica Armour, and Bernadette Emerson.

Elizabeth MacCrellish, who saw the embers of my potential and blew them into a steady flame. Her faith in me and my teaching has been life changing and made this book possible.

Sweet Land Farm, our abundant CSA, that kept my family well fed so that our garden could rest while I grew a book! Their produce and flowers are found on several of the pages of *Reinvention*!

My thrifting hero Kate Lunde, who introduced me to salvaged coffee sacks and then gifted me with her stash of rescued materials when she moved out of the country.

Tillie Ellinwood for her helping hands and beautiful listening ears.

Lizzy House and Pixie Campbell for their love and light.

Joe Frisino and Viviane Galloway, our dearest friends who transformed into a whirlwind editing team when I needed them most.

Laura Nelkin, my right hand girlfriend and midnight pep talker… who urged me forward each step of the way.

Deborah Donenfeld, for being the older sister I never had and for bringing her discerning eye and experience behind the lens to each image I wanted to create.

My dear family and lovely friends who enthusiastically jumped onto the pages of this book by modeling. I am so proud of Dani Diciaccio, Erica Naylor, Ayla, Naia, Noemi, Sylvan, Izzy, Ursula, and Parker. You made each project come alive with your beauty and playfulness.

Amy, my aunt, best friend, confidant, and daily cheerleader.

My mom, whose loving presence in this book is felt on every page… from the backdrop of her barn, to the textiles we researched together during one late night after another. She provided me with the most creative and colorful childhood and then gave me the skills and tools to do the same for my children.

Above all I am thankful to my sweet and tender husband, Sunny, who always knew I could do it and never let me doubt myself. And to our tremendous children, Sylvan and Noemi, who teach me every day what is truly important: to love deeply, make thoughtful choices, and be creative.

Table of Contents

CAFÉ MAYA

Introduction

re·in·ven·tion \\,rē-in-'ven(t)- shən\\

noun: Something new created from that which already exists.

This book is a guide to working with some of my favorite rescued materials. I believe in using what is readily available and abundant to transform it into something surprising and new. As a reinventor I love the challenge of making "something out of nothing"; tossing a t-shirt into a top hat and magically pulling out a string of recycled jersey blossoms (see page 74)!

I come from a long line of reinventors. My grandfather built our family house with thrift, ingenuity, and what was on hand. It was the first passive solar-heated house on Long Island (circa 1940s). Twenty-five years later, as a small child, my mother and I combed the thrift stores of San Francisco's Mission district. In the creative spirit of the '60s and early '70s, outdated and discarded clothing became our re-created artful wardrobe and old furniture was repurposed into new.

Today, as technology advances and the pace of our lives quickens, we are feeling the pull of age-old traditions that promise to connect us to a slower and simpler time. We long to feel a deeper connection to the food we eat, the spaces we inhabit, and even in the clothes we wear.

This pull has given rise to the vibrant Do-It-Yourself movement that continues to gain momentum as an ever-growing number of makers, crafters, and urban homesteaders bring sustainable living into their own back yards. Fueled by the challenges of our times, we are reinventing the customs and practices of our forebears with the knowledge, tools, and skills of today.

Out of this movement a sewing renaissance has been set in motion. Sewing provides a way for us to slow down and incorporate creativity, utility, and independence into our lives. There is a deep sense of satisfaction in making something that becomes an integral part of our daily lives.

As much as sewing is a tradition, so is creating with what's on hand. We have only to look at the resourcefulness of our ancestors and millions of people all over the world who live by the familiar adage of "waste not, want not." Today, this philosophy is also a green choice. Working with rescued materials is a concrete response to the reality of overflowing landfills, depleted resources, and a contaminated environment.

Whether out of economic necessity or the pleasure in *making something out of nothing,* sewing with used fabric is a timeless model of resourcefulness.

When we depend less on industrially produced consumer goods, we can live in quiet places. Our bodies become vigorous; we discover the serenity of living with the rhythms of the earth. ~ ALICIA BAY LAUREL

Reinvention: Sewing with Rescued Materials focuses on seven textiles that I find inspiring, abundant, and easily rescued. The chapters are organized by material: linen, burlap, wool, jersey, vintage, mailers, and denim.

At the beginning of each material's chapter are interesting details, history, sourcing, deconstruction techniques, tips, and a brief discussion of their environmental impact. The more I became familiar with these textiles, the better I was able to understand their strengths as well as address their challenges and incorporate them into my designs. I often asked these questions: How can I best honor the material? Is it something that will get regular use? Will I enjoy the making process?

There are 28 projects in this book, from a rugged burlap log carrier to an insulating wool lunch sack. I hope you'll find them inspiring, useful, and a pleasure to make. To add an element of personalization, I often incorporate simple printing into my sewing, and I am excited to share this finishing touch with you. Stenciling templates and thorough instructions are provided, as well as encouragement to make up your own designs.

Although the projects are of varying skill levels and completion times, all are based on simple techniques. Ease of execution equals success, whether you are a seasoned refashioner or a novice sewer. With *Reinvention* I offer you guidelines and patterns, but ultimately the size, shape, and color of each rescued piece inform the final outcome. If you listen carefully, the fabric will tell you what it wants to be. I invite you to listen with me.

My Sewing Story

Sewing is an accessible and intimate form of creativity that often catches hold of the seamstress and weaves its magic into the chapters of one's life. Many of us have a sewing story—a history that began with our first stitched projects and the person who taught us to thread a needle. It often evolves into the relationships we build with our sewing machines and the memories of project successes and fizzles. Some of our stories may have been on hold for many years or maybe they are just beginning . . .

I grew up during the '70s when the "Back to the Land" movement was in full swing. Sewing was considered a way of being resourceful and innovative. Improvisation was respected, whereas following rules was considered too safe and boring. My mother paid heed to this credo and the pinch in her checkbook as she sewed throughout my childhood. I know I absorbed her philosophy as I played with buttons and fabric scraps. She made lots of my clothes, curtains, and bedding . . . often revamping thrift store finds. We never went to fabric stores, often reinventing sheets, tablecloths, and Indian cotton tapestries. Patterns were never used, only daring and risk taking. I made simple hand-stitched toys as soon as I could hold a needle, but it wasn't until I took a Home Ec class in junior high that I got comfortable with a sewing machine. The class was tedious for someone with my background, but the outcome was pure liberation when I discovered the power of a sewing machine. I proceeded to peg every pair of jeans in my closet. That was the beginning of my wardrobe refashioning.

When I went off to college I decided that all of my clothing would be thrifted or handmade. I bought a turn-of-the-century Singer sewing machine that could only be used with a hand crank. Because it needed no electricity, it offered me the freedom to sew anywhere. I remember taking it out to my back yard and stitching under the avocado tree.

Turning the wheel with one hand and guiding fabric with the other ensured slow and steady sewing and encouraged mostly small projects or alterations. This was about the time that I set foot in my first real fabric store. I was 20 years old. I had no money, but would go there just to lovingly finger the bolts of varied prints. When I was ready to learn a little bit more about construction, I drove over the mountain to my mom's and the original sewing machine I had learned on. She taught me how to trace favorite clothing onto newspaper and re-create it with fabric. One of my first dresses was made out of a white flannel sheet that I dyed purple. I still have the pattern I drafted for that piece so many years ago (and the dress!).

Many dresses followed; often times they were created for a special occasion and are steeped in rich memories. They each have a story of where and when they were created, but none so significant as my wedding dress and my husband's wedding attire. With a desire to use a specialty fabric and a limited budget, it seemed obvious that I would need to be the seamstress. This was long before sourcing fabric and supplies on the Internet was a possibility. Woven into the memories of my wedding is the search for the undyed hemp fabric that I was determined to sew my dress out of. Ironically, I found it at that first fabric store I had entered in my old college town, Santa Cruz's very own Harts Fabric. How wild that it's now possible to shop at Harts from anywhere in the world thanks to the Internet.

For the next decade my sewing projects were focused on my home and growing family. Nesting and motherhood were intertwined with thread and needle from the very beginning. I sewed everything from functional pieces to wand, wings, and fairy magic for my children. Discovering the world of crafters and creatives online offered community, conversation, and a platform to share and promote what I make. Offering you this book is the next chapter in my sewing story. ■

ON THE JOB. ON THE LEVEL.™
J48 / 40-0567
OLFA ROTARY CUTTER
DEAN
MADE IN CHINA

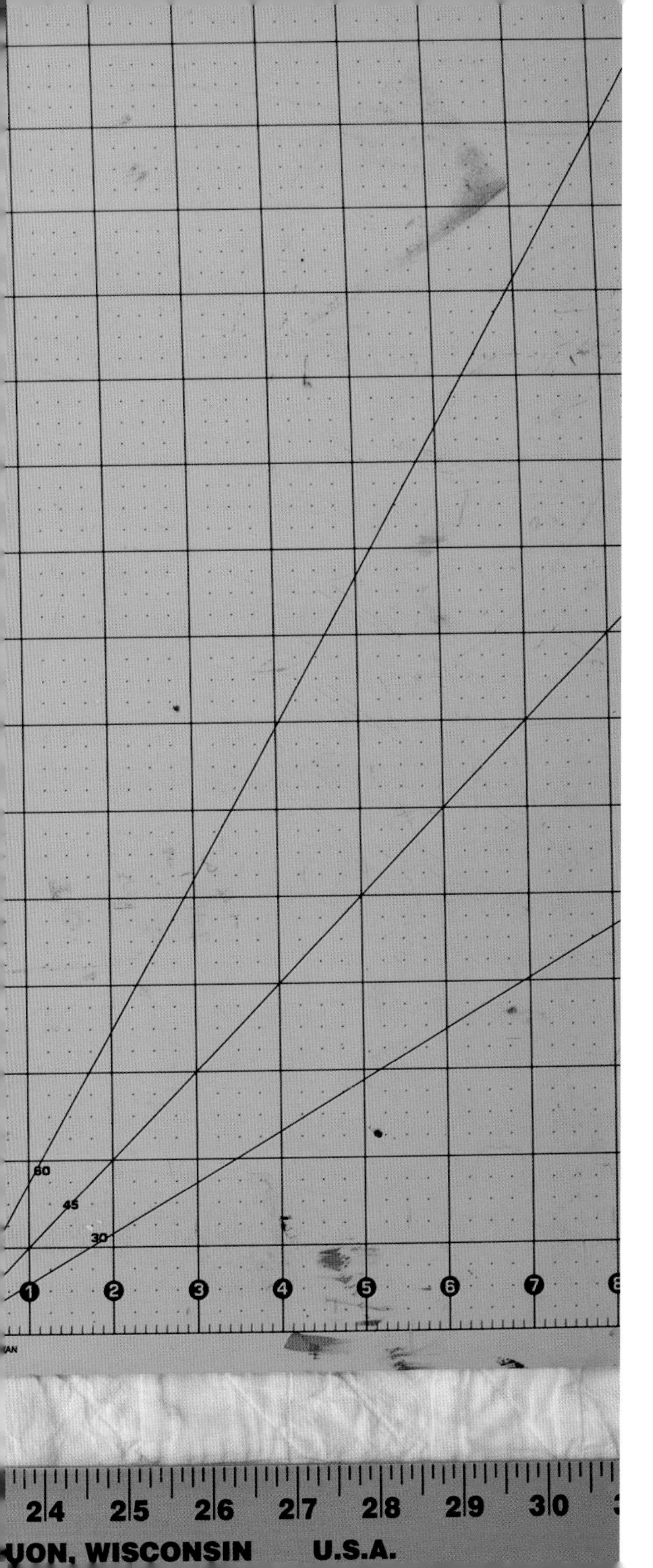

CHAPTER 1

SEWING BASICS

As with any skill, the more you practice, the easier it becomes. I've learned some tricks from years of sewing and have included them here, but I want to pass on something far more important than techniques: I offer you an invitation to create your own rules. This will inevitably include making a few blunders. Mistakes shouldn't be feared or avoided; they are wonderful opportunities to learn and often lead to new ideas and designs. A fantastic benefit of using thrifted material is the small price tag. It's much easier to take creative risks when financial loss isn't hanging over us as we cut into a piece of fabric. I encourage you to try out the projects in each section with the hope that you'll launch into your own versions and iterations as you gain confidence and familiarity with each material and your toolbox.

Tools

Having the right tool for the job makes all the difference in the world, but this doesn't mean that you need fancy and expensive gadgets. Here are the basics you'll find at my work table:

Scissors: It's always nice to have several kinds of scissors on hand, but only two are really necessary:

- Basic fabric scissors
- Small embroidery scissors for snipping threads while at the machine (nail scissors work just fine)

Rotary blade: This specialty fabric cutter resembles a pizza wheel. Use it against the edge of a sturdy ruler on a mat for straight cuts. It makes for quick and easy cutting but should always be used with care. The blades are exceptionally sharp and should be replaced the moment a swift, clean cut becomes challenging. Make it a habit to put up the safety shield every time you set down the blade.

Cutting mat: Most mats are marked with a grid to help in fabric placement. They're made of a special material that is self-healing and keeps blades from dulling quickly. Invest in the largest one your wallet and space can afford. The bigger the size, the easier it is to work with large pieces of fabric (or coffee sacks!).

Rulers: Having a variety of different widths and lengths is helpful; here are my two must-haves with a third option thrown in:

1. An **acrylic see-through grid ruler** is found in the quilting section of most fabric stores. It's a perfect partner to the grid on large cutting mats and makes it easy to draw and mark perpendicular lines.
2. A **steel yardstick** is useful for cutting all but the smallest pieces of fabric. It's heavy, sturdy, and won't get nicked by a rotary cutter. Look for one at your local hardware store, which often sells them at a fraction of the cost of fabric shop prices.
3. The **sewing gauge ruler** has a sliding indicator to mark a specific measurement. Although it's the least necessary item in my toolbox, the handy size and clear markings make it helpful for repeat measurements on hems and seam allowances. It's also great for spacing tucks, pleats, and buttonholes.

Measuring tape: This flexible tape is used for measuring circumferences and soft, curved things.

Pencils: Keep a pencil handy at all times. They're the best writing implement for taking measurements and notes that might need adjustments, making patterns, and even drawing on the wrong side of fabric.

Tailor's chalk: This classic marking tool is often used by tailors. Draw on fabric and then rub it off with a damp cloth.

Water soluble pens: Used to mark directly on fabric and helpful if you need a sharper line than chalk provides.

Pin cushion and pins: Keep several pin cushions filled with pins so there's always a pin handy when you need one and so you have a place to tuck the pins you pull out.

Thimble: Protects fingers when hand-sewing through many layers of fabric.

Seam ripper: This pointed tool with a small blade removes unwanted stitches and opens buttonholes. I like to have one by my machine and another where I cut fabric.

Thread: All-purpose thread is suitable for most projects unless otherwise stated. As much as I love the look of vintage spools of thread, they're not recommend for everyday sewing because of their fragility. Investing in new and good-quality thread keeps a sewing machine running smoothly and keeps seams from breaking.

Terms

Backstitch: At the beginning and end of a seam, always reverse for several stitches and then continue to the start or finish point. This is sometimes called *backtack* and is the term for locking the bottom and top threads together to prevent unraveling. It's a good habit to get into for every seam, unless otherwise stated.
Baste: A temporary running stitch used to hold two pieces of fabric together. Use the longest stitch length.
Topstitch: Straight stitching sewn directly to the right side of a project, often parallel to a seam or edge of fabric. It provides stability or is used for decorative purposes.
Edgestitch: Just like topstitching except it is sewn as close to the edge as possible, often ⅛" from the edge.
Seam allowance: The fabric between the raw edge and the seam.
Wrong side/right side: The side of the fabric that is visible on the finished project is the right side. This is obvious with a printed material, but some fabrics (such as linen) appear the same on either side. Denim has the ability to look very different depending on which side is used, and the reverse side is used frequently for the projects in this book.

Techniques

Making handles: Fold a fabric rectangle in half lengthwise and press with a hot iron. Open and fold each side just to the crease. Fold in half again. The crease is on one side; the folded edges are on the other. Press with an iron once more. Sew a straight stitch along the edge of each side.
Clipping curves: To reduce bulk and create a flat seam on a curve, snip little v-shaped cuts into the seam allowance after sewing. A concave curve only requires the slits to be snipped. Remember to not get too close to the seam line or you'll cut through the stitches.

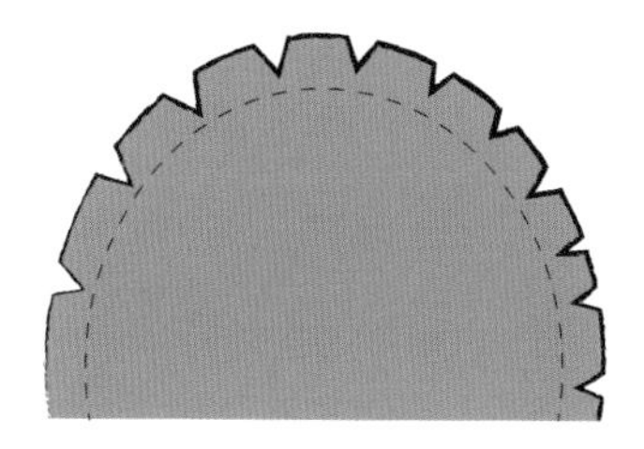

CLIPPING CURVES

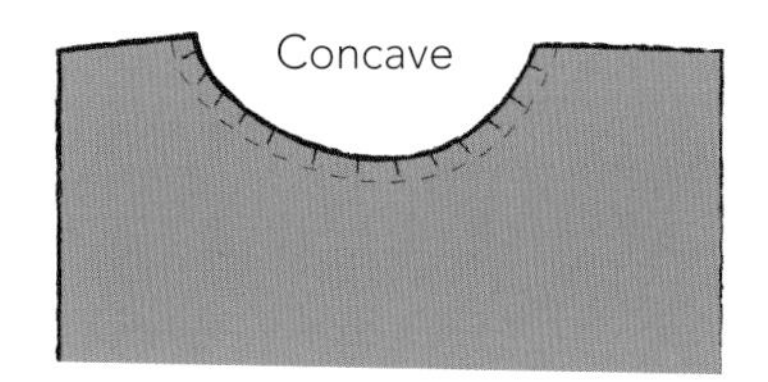

Clipping corners: Whenever a corner is sewn, clip off the excess seam allowance (a little triangle of fabric) at the point where the seams meet. Be careful not to cut into the seam line. When the project is turned right side out the corner will be nice and crisp.

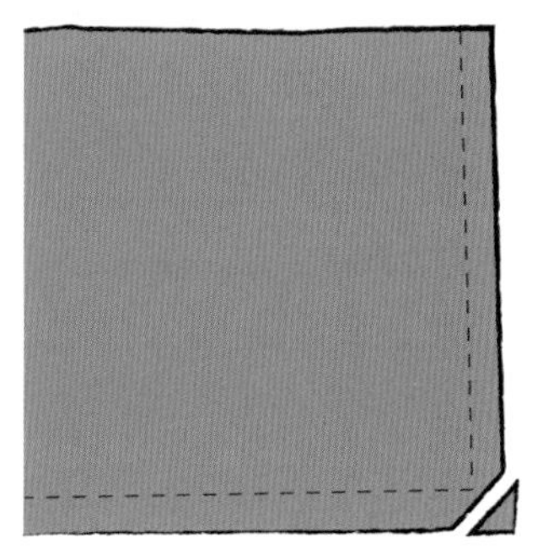

CLIPPING A CORNER

DIY circle templates: It's easy to create a perfect circle of your desired size with nothing more than a ruler, a pen, and a piece of paper large enough to fit the diameter of your circle. A *diameter* is the measurement directly across the center of the circle. A *radius* is half of the diameter

1 Fold a piece of paper in half twice so that it's folded into quarters. Lay the paper so that the two folded sides are on the left and bottom.

STEP 1

2 Use a ruler to mark the length of the radius of your circle on both those sides. For example, a 12" circle has a 6" radius.

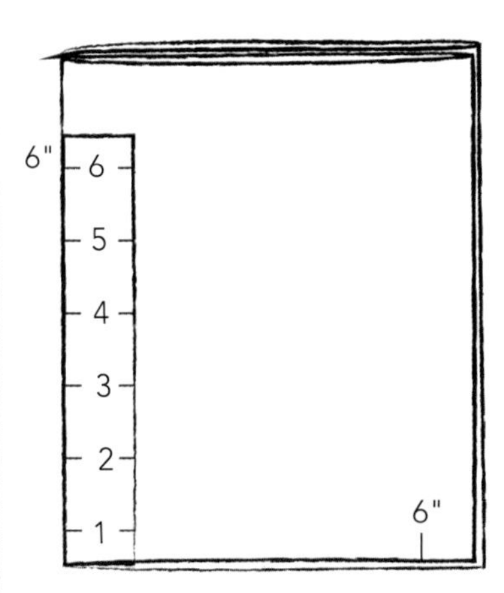

STEP 2

3 Keep the ruler's bottom point exactly where the two sides meet and slowly move it from one radius mark to the other. Draw dots every ½" or so.

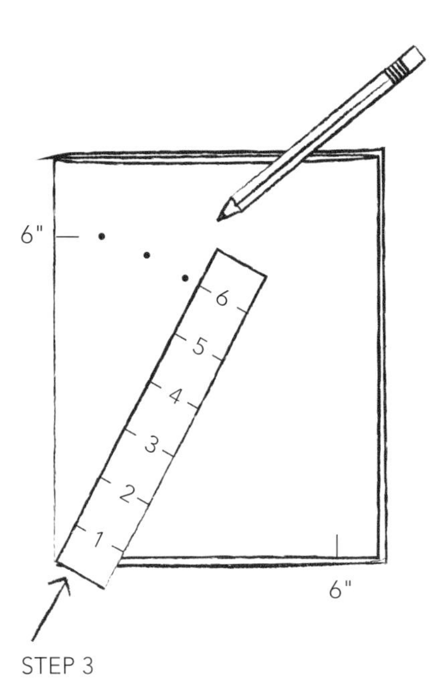

STEP 3

4 Connect the dots and cut along that line. Open folded paper to reveal a perfect 12" circle.

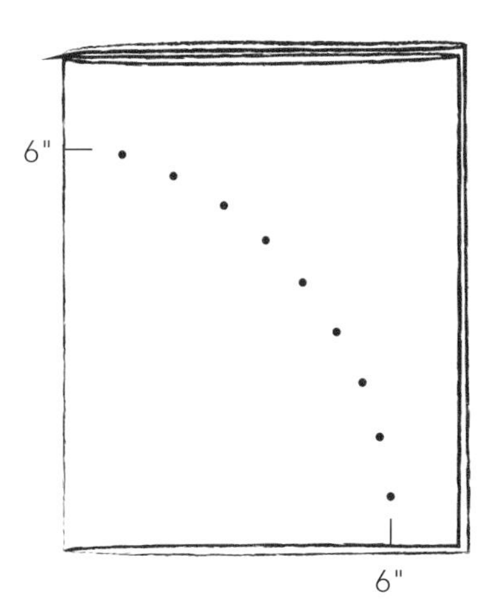

STEP 4

Gathers and ruffles: The general rule for gathering is to cut the fabric two-and-a-half times longer than the desired final measurement. Set the sewing machine for straight stitching and adjust it to the longest stitch length.

1 Stitch along the fabric ½" in from the edge. Leave tails at least 4" long when you snip your top and bobbin threads. Unlike when you make a regular seam, when you make a gathering stitch, don't backstitch to lock threads.

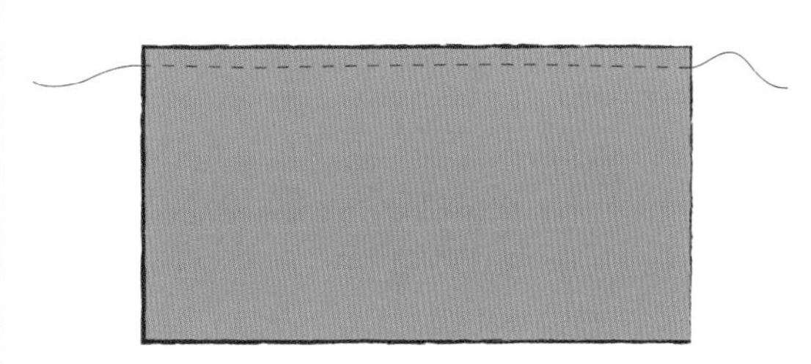

STEP 1

2 Stitch another row about ¼" in from the fabric edge. Again, leave long tails when you snip your thread. There will be two parallel rows of long straight stitches.

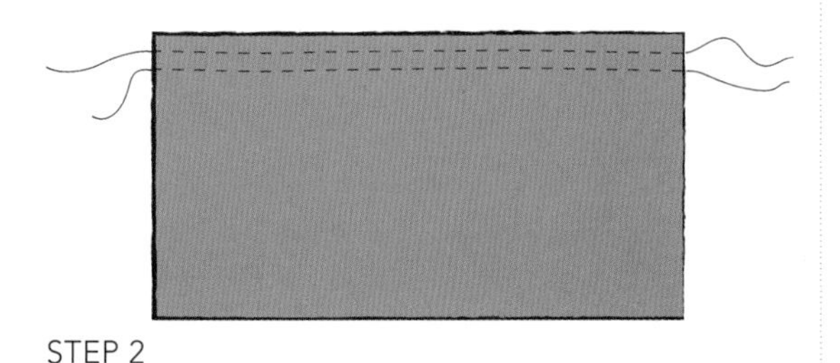

STEP 2

3 At the other end of your fabric *gently* pull on the two *top* threads. Slide your fabric along these threads to form ruffles. Continue pulling. Adjust and even out the ruffles as you go. When it's gathered evenly along the whole edge and is the finished length you want, tie a knot on both ends. Add this gather to any project.

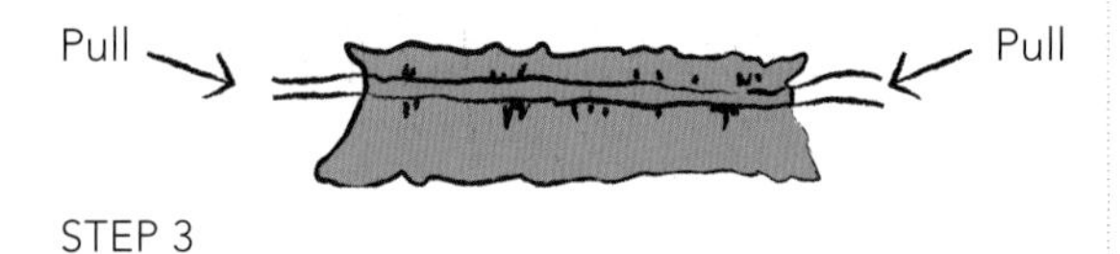

STEP 3

A *ruffle* is often just a narrow strip that has been gathered. It can be sewn directly to the right side of fabric. Stitch over the seam of gathering stitches.

Pin tucks: Add dimension and interest to the surface of fabric with this very simple manipulation.

1 Draw a line directly on the right side of your fabric (with chalk). Fold on the line and press.

2 Sew ⅛" from the edge along the entire line remembering to backstitch at the beginning and end. This is one pin tuck.

So easy! Pin tucks look wonderful in groups spaced evenly apart and all the same length. They're also intriguing to space randomly or in different lengths. It's helpful to draw all of your lines first and then begin sewing.

Tips

Get to know your sewing machine. Read through the manual and keep it handy for reference. Seek online resources for any unknowns and questions. Purchase or take out of the library a general sewing handbook. See the "Resources" section at the end of the book.

Keep scissors sharp. Only use them for fabric. The blades will dull if used on any other material (such as paper). Putting a "fabric only" label on the handle is helpful. Cutting should be easy and not involve strain or the need for pressure when slicing through fabric. Most fabric stores can direct you to a local scissor sharpener.

Change sewing machine needles often. Many machine issues can be fixed with a new needle.

Measure twice, cut once. This old saying will save you lots of time and wasted fabric.

Keep your iron handy. From pressing seams to crisping up edges, a hot iron is indispensible for successful sewing. Iron your yardage before you cut it, and press your stitches after you sew them. Every project will be enhanced if you become friends with your iron.

Have multiples on hand. Invest in several pairs of your most used tools.

Being creative is not so much the desire to do something as the listening to that which wants to be done: the dictation of the materials. ~ ANNI ALBERS

NEEDLES
UNITY
20 Nickel Plated SAFETY PINS
Made in England

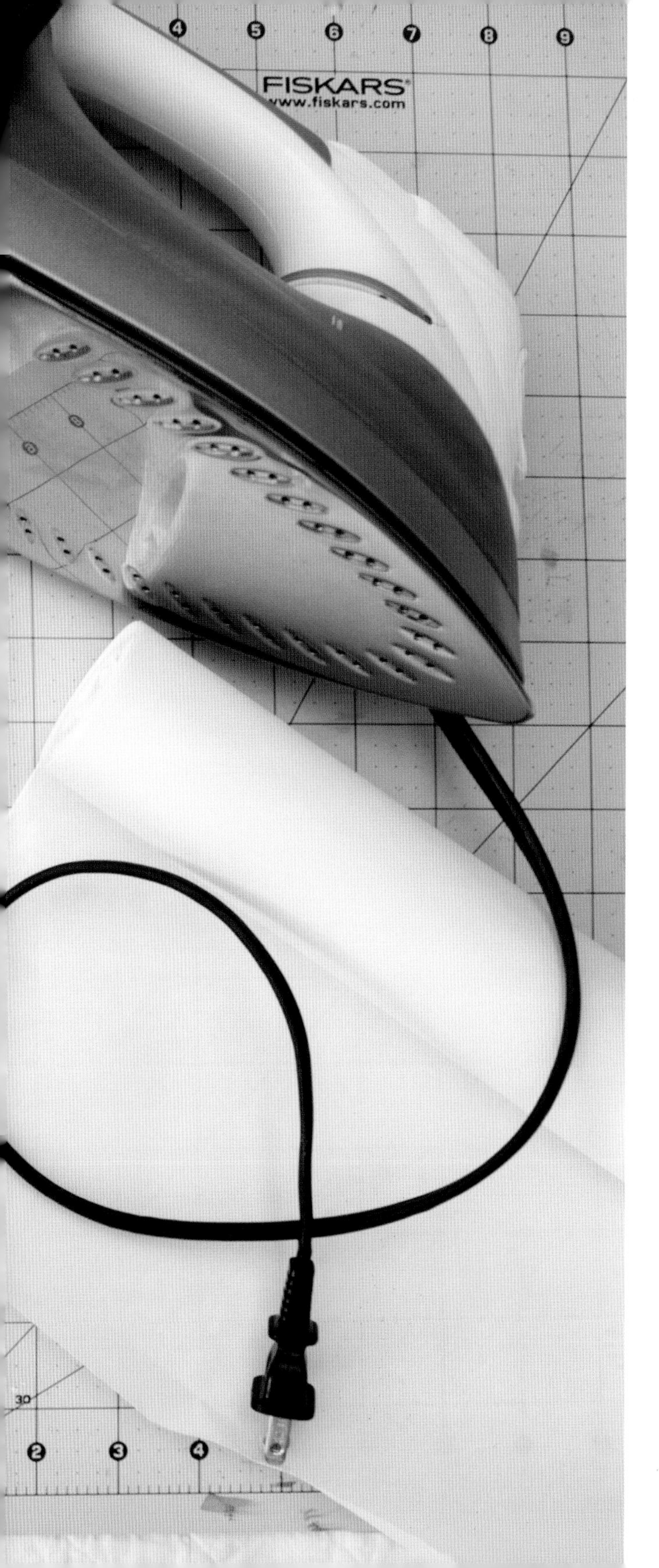

CHAPTER 2

PRINTING BASICS

For years, I completed sewing projects with a vague feeling that something was missing. I wished to add a part of me that went beyond the seams. When I discovered printing on fabric, I knew I had found that final piece. By embellishing with your own hand, you add a layer of yourself onto the fabric that can't be achieved with manufactured notions. In sharing these basics on stenciling and stamping, I hope to make the process simple and accessible for everyone. I've included my stencil designs for inspiration and as a teaching tool, but please consider them only as launch pads for your own creativity.

Freezer Paper Printing

By using an inexpensive kitchen material, freezer paper, anyone has the ability to create unique designs and prints on fabric. The results are similar to screen printing, except each design is one-of-a-kind and very few materials are needed to begin. You can find freezer paper at most grocery stores in the plastic bag aisle. It has a glossy side that has been traditionally used for wrapping food for freezer storage. That glossy side is where the magic lies. When ironed to fabric it sticks and creates a strong seal, making it a perfect medium for stenciling on textiles.

SUPPLIES

Freezer paper
Scissors
Craft knife
Self-healing cutting mat
Textile paints
Paint brushes in a variety of sizes (inexpensive foam brushes are especially effective and can be used again and again)
Iron and ironing board
Fabric with a tight weave, such as cotton or linen
Toothpicks
Tweezers

BASIC INSTRUCTIONS

1 Draw the design directly onto the matte side of freezer paper. If you're using a template, place the paper on top of the template with the shiny side facing the design. Trace the design onto the dull side of the paper. (Hint: Although freezer paper has some transparency, working with a light box or taping it to a window makes the tracing easier.)

2 Place the freezer paper onto a cutting mat and use a craft knife to cut out the design. Set aside the cut-out pieces.

3 Place the paper with the design on the fabric with the shiny side down. Make sure the design is exactly where you want it.

4 Protect your painting surface and project by ironing a separate piece of freezer paper to the underside of the fabric as well. Cut a piece slightly larger than the design and place it shiny side up directly under the fabric where the design will be located.

5 Set the iron to medium-high heat. When it's nice and hot, hold the iron directly above the paper and place it down flat to set the paper. Always seal all of the design at once with a light "stamp" or two of the iron. If you move the iron back and forth across the paper *before* setting it, a corner or flap of the design is sure to fold over and

will not adhere to fabric as well once it has touched the iron. Make sure there is a firm seal on every part of the stencil design. You now have your fabric sandwiched between two pieces of paper and are ready to add color.

6 Apply a small amount of paint to the paper next to the design. First lightly move it in gentle sweeping motions to the center of the design on the fabric. Try not to stroke the brush toward the paper; if you do you might inadvertently push some paint under the edge. Traditional stencil painting calls for a stipple motion (light up-and-down tapping of a brush). I've found that fabric prefers a light stroke instead, especially when painting across a large surface.

7 Hold it up to a window or light periodically to make sure you're not leaving any parts undone. The light shines through the design and highlights any areas that need more paint.

8 Allow the paint to dry to the touch. If you can't wait, a hair dryer does the job swiftly.

9 Remove the freezer paper by tearing it away from the fabric with care. Tweezers are helpful for pulling off any small bits of paper that remain stuck to the fabric.

10 Admire! It's amazing how such a simple process can have such stunning results.

But wait, are there some spots that look less crisp than others? Perhaps an edge that smudged a tiny bit? The tiny, hard point of a toothpick is a fantastic tool for touch-ups. Dip just the tip into paint and hold it like a mini pencil to refine any rough spots.

11 After you have completed the touch-ups and the paint is dry, heat set with an iron. Place a thin cloth between your work and the iron.

ADDING COMPLEXITY

A stencil in its simplest form is a silhouette. The math pillows in the "Linen" chapter are a perfect example. To add details and definition, you can play with the positive and negative spaces. The degree of intricacy that can be achieved is determined by the steadiness of your hand and the depth of your patience. In my workshops we always use white fabric swatches to mimic the white freezer paper. If you think of the paper as the fabric, what you cut away will be the painted image. Cutting on a dark surface can simulate the color of paint and help you visualize this concept. To add more detail or create outlines, incorporate "islands" of freezer paper within a cut-out area as in the following example of creating an outlined leaf:

1 Cut out a leaf's silhouette from a square of freezer paper.

2 Take that cut-out leaf and trim it down slightly to a smaller size with a craft knife or sharp scissors.

3 Iron the square of freezer paper with the leaf silhouette to the fabric.

4 Place the trimmed-down freezer paper leaf in the center of the silhouette and iron it in place.

5 Paint over the design for a leaf outline.

NOTE: To add even more definition, cut out veins within the smaller leaf before ironing it down.

Tips

- **Sharp knife:** A dull blade tears paper and causes lots of trouble. Always change blades when they don't slice through paper with ease.
- **Test fabric:** The same paint responds differently to each unique surface. Take into account the fabric color and the looseness of the weave. Lighter colors of fabric generally take prints best, and a tightly woven material makes the cleanest print.

- **Printing stencils with an inkjet printer:** A clever way to transfer your design directly to freezer paper is to scan the image and then print it onto an 8½" × 11" piece of freezer paper. Cut the freezer paper to size and, because it's often sold in a roll, press it under a stack of books to flatten it. Feed it into the printer so that the ink lands on the matte side. This technique is especially exciting if you like typography. You can print any font on your computer directly onto freezer paper for your next printing adventure.
- **Inverse printing:** Save the cut-outs of any of your designs to use as the inverse or negative of your original print. Cut out a square or circle from freezer paper to create a frame. Insert the inverse "scrap" into the center. Iron and paint for a new look.
- **Label freezer-paper islands:** If there are more than three "islands" of a similar shape (flower petals are a good example) give each one a number before you begin to cut. Jot down a corresponding number next to it on the freezer paper that remains. When it's time to iron down the island pieces, you'll know just where to place them.

Stamping

Printing on fabric with stamps is instantly gratifying. Having a variety of stamp pads with textile ink invites you to explore found objects in nature and around the house. Use an old t-shirt or fabric squares for testing and experimenting. Unlike the single image of most stencils, stamping cries out for a pattern or repeated images. Some of my favorite found objects include the following:

- Buttons
- Spools
- Corks
- Pencil erasers
- Bottle caps

Some favorite natural objects are

- Walnut halves (a secret heart emerges with each stamp!)
- Dried flower pods (poppies make a wonderful impression)
- Small leaves
- Shells
- Eucalyptus pods

Small alphabet stamps are always a good choice, as they lend themselves to little monograms or favorite words. Of course, ready-made stamps, as well as materials to carve your own stamps, are widely available at all craft stores.

SUGGESTIONS FOR PRINTING ON *REINVENTION* MATERIALS

Material	Notes
Linen	Perfect for stamping and stenciling.
Burlap	Stamping small items on the loose weave is challenging. Stenciling works well, but isn't as crisp as on a tightly woven fabric.
Jersey	Perfect for stamping and stenciling.
Wool	Stamping and stenciling are easier on wool suiting than blankets. Textile paint often adheres to the top of the wool fibers awkwardly. Definitely test a small swatch first.
Vintage	Often the fabric is tightly woven cotton or linen, which is perfect for stamping and stenciling.
Mailers	Irons can't be used with Dupont™ Tyvek® mailers, so freezer paper stenciling isn't an option. Stamps using ink pads made for plastic are recommended.
Denim	Perfect for stamping and stenciling.

NOTE: Whenever possible, test the type of printing on your chosen material before embellishing a project.

CHAPTER 3

LINEN

The early Egyptians called it "woven moonlight." With its soft drape, smooth texture, and luminous ivory color this ancient textile has represented purity and strength for thousands of years. Linen is derived from the fibers of flax, one of the oldest agricultural plants in the world. It has withstood the test of time because of its inherent resiliency and versatility. More than twice as strong as cotton, linen has always been revered for its breathability, absorbency, and ability to soften over time. It's the super textile of the natural world.

History

Linen was the very first plant-based woven textile in the world. Ten thousand-year-old fabric made from flax has been discovered in Neolithic Swiss lake dwellings, and dyed flax fibers were found in prehistoric caves in Georgia. Thousands of years later, the Egyptians shrouded their mummies in its long-lasting fibers. It has been said that when the tomb of Tutankhamen was opened in 1922, the linen curtains endured the sudden exposure whereas the other fabrics disintegrated. Linen's ability to remain pristinely preserved has been well documented. The British Museum of London's collection of ancient Egyptian linen is breathtaking (see the "Resources" section for details on how you can access it online).

Although today's linen is grown in many parts of the world, the highest-quality linen is produced in Western Europe much as it was in the beginning. It is most often harvested by hand in small crops. This accounts for the fabric's high price and is why it is considered a luxury fabric today.

Sourcing

Head to your nearest thrift store or consignment shop for linen clothing and tablecloths. Linen yardage can be costly. Using deconstructed clothing is not only a money saver, but it offers opportunities for a wide variety of colors, prints, and weights that you can never find at a fabric store. Go directly to the women's better clothing section and keep an eye out for skirts and dresses, which offer the most fabric and are commonly made out of linen. Business suits and pants are also favorite finds with interesting pockets and detail work that are always exciting to salvage and incorporate into something new.

Deconstructing

- All clothing gets similar treatment. Use a seam ripper to open up side seams.
- Remove pockets for a multitude of reuses.
- Button-down shirts offer up their buttons as well as the placket with button holes.
- Keep an iron at hand to smooth out creases from seams.

Tips

- Linen is laundered easily. Most methods are suitable, but because it absorbs moisture so well, line drying is recommended as an especially green choice, rather than long tumbles in the dryer.
- Linen is known for its soft, wrinkled appearance, but can be ironed easily for a smoother, crisp look if you press it while the linen is damp. Pull it off the line just before it's fully dry to maximize its pressing potential.
- To create a frayed edge, pull threads out of the weave one at a time. The true straight edge of the weave will emerge. Trim off any parts that are uneven.

Environmental Impact

Although not perfect, linen has a modest environmental footprint and is considered a natural and fairly green textile. The whole flax plant is used, leaving no waste. Flax has a short growing season , which minimizes the need for and use of pesticides and fertilizers. It requires less energy for processing than most textiles, and the processing uses little water. The European Union ensures safe working conditions with fair wages for the cultivation, spinning, and weaving process of linen, so knowing the origin of your fabric is important.

STORY SCARF

STORY SCARF

Finished Dimensions: 6" × 59"

The story scarf originated as a simple teaching tool in my Reinvention classes to introduce ruffles, pleats, and other embellishment techniques. The scarves are reminiscent of early-American samplers. I was astounded by the creativity and unique interpretation they inspired. These scarves beg for improvisation and collage as much as they provide a framework for displaying meaningful and sentimental textiles. In essence, they are one-of-a-kind, wearable stories. Adding a ready-made pocket from old clothing incorporates utility and function, which is always a bonus.

NOTE: As you're looking for ways to incorporate meaning into a scarf, seek out favorite items of clothing from a loved one. Consider some of these possibilities: pieces from a parent's favorite apron, a grandfather's familiar flannel shirt, a grandmother's lace handkerchief, children's clothing that's been outgrown, and vintage notions.

SUPPLIES

- Deconstructed linen clothing in complementary colors and patterns; pant legs are especially useful for making scarves because of their perfect length and width
- Bits of lace or ribbons
- Favorite items of clothing from a loved one
- Flexible measuring tape (optional but helpful)
- Scissors
- Ruler

Cut

1 First, decide on the width of your scarf. The one shown in the sample began with 7"-wide pieces. This is a comfortable size for wrapping around your neck, but, if you enjoy skinny scarves or prefer extra-wide scarves, please do experiment. After you've determined the width, cut various lengths from your fabric selection to that width.

NOTE: If you'd like to add gathers or pleats, cut at least two lengths that are several inches wider than your base width.

2 Cut a pocket from an old shirt or the back pocket from a pair of pants if you'd like your scarf to have a pocket.

Design Ideas

1 If you want to use gathers or pleats, consider these options for the wider squares:

- *Gathers* add dimension. Using the instructions in Chapter 2, gather the bottom and the top of a section of an extra-wide piece of linen until it is uniformly the same width as the rest of the scarf pieces (7" in the case of the sample).

- *Pin tucks* create lovely texture. Refer to Chapter 2 and create horizontal pin tucks on a 7"-wide piece of linen. Alternatively you can sew vertical pin tucks using an extra-wide section of linen and then cut any excess until it also measures 7".

2 To add a touch of femininity and whimsy create some *raw-edged ruffles*. Stitch up several to be added at a later stage by cutting a 1" strip that is more than double the width of the scarf (16" in the case of the sample). Follow the instructions in Chapter 2 to create the ruffle. From a design standpoint, ruffles look best when one ruffle stands alone or when you create bunches of three.

3 Stencil or stamp a section.

4 Add embroidery or fancy machine stitches with contrasting thread.

Collage

1 Drape a measuring tape around your neck to get a sense of the length you'd like the final scarf to be. The sample scarf measured 7" × 60" before it was sewn.

2 Lay out all of your pieces for the front of the scarf on the floor or a large table. Enjoy the process of finding a combination that feels just right. Keep in mind that the bottom 16" is the most visible, so that is where the embellished pieces should be focused. Any pockets work best about 7" or 8" from the bottom. Don't forget to face them with the closed side aimed towards the bottom of the scarf! The center portion of each scarf should be kept minimal as it will be wrapped around the neck.

3 The back of the scarf needs only to be simple long sections of linen stitched together to match the dimensions of the front. Measure to make sure that you have enough for the back side. Long strips from pant legs work perfectly for the backing. Cut more linen if necessary.

Put It All Together

1 Sew the scarf front. Place the sections right side to right side and stitch along the width using the presser foot as a seam allowance guide.

2 Turn to the wrong side and press open all seams.

3 Add lace or ribbon and attach ruffles. These notions look especially nice covering the seam where two pieces are joined.

4 Repeat the same steps for the back: Sew the pieces with right sides together along the width and press open the seams.

5 Lay the front and back on top of each other with the right sides facing. Trim to ensure the front and back are the same size and pin them together. Stitch around the entire perimeter using the presser foot as a seam allowance guide. Leave a 4" opening in the center of the scarf for turning.

6 Clip off all four corners taking care not to get too close to the stitches.

7 Turn the scarf right side out and poke out the corners with a chopstick or the eraser end of a pencil. Press. Pin the opening closed and sew it with an invisible seam. It's ready to wear!

Variation: Use a section of linen containing a pocket with a flap as a clever way to "fasten" both scarf ends together, as shown at the beginning of the book.

Connecting the Stitches

Favorite and familiar clothing of those closest to us evokes memories whether we're looking at old photographs or standing before a closet. It is as if the spirit and vitality of the person who owned them are woven into the very fabric.

The first time I taught my workshop on how to make scarves from deconstructed pants and tops, I realized the depth of emotion that cloth could elicit. I had requested participants to bring used clothing for deconstruction. One woman courageously brought her father's old favorite shirt that he had sported every weekend for gardening and cooking. It had been several years since he had passed, but this tattered old gray shirt felt very much alive. I could see by the tenderness with which she held it how much she loved and missed him. Transforming it into something wearable felt deeply significant, and I was honored to be a part of the process. Determining what part of it to use and how to cut into it was the most emotionally challenging step and took some time. When she was ready we were silent as the scissors took their first snip. This was sacred sewing, and we both sensed it. That segment of her father's shirt became the backing of the scarf where it would be closest to the wearer. This thoughtful and sensitive sewer was making the scarf for her mother—connecting her family through stitches, memories, and love. Reinventing simply adds soul to what we sew. ■

ARITHMETIC PILLOWS

ARITHMETIC PILLOWS

Finished Dimensions: 14" × 14"

An envelope pillow is the quintessential beginning sewing project, but it's just as popular with experienced sewers. There's really no better way to give a room a quick update than fresh cushions, and an envelope backing is as practical as it is fast. These math pillows offer high graphic impact and are a perfect first stencil experience. Use them for a design statement or to make adding and subtracting fun for young mathematicians. They stimulate the use of concrete objects for a more sensorial approach to early equations. Addition and subtraction will come to life when you toss a few of these pillows on a child's bed or in your living space.

NOTE: The instructions call for a 14" insert, but you can easily customize the size to whatever pillow inserts you have on hand or however large your linen pieces are. Calculate one extra inch on both sides for whatever size pillow form is used. Linen skirts and dresses are popular thrift store items that yield lots of fabric for larger cushions, so keep an eye out for them.

SUPPLIES

- 15" × 15" piece linen for pillow front
- 2 15" × 11" pieces linen for pillow back
- Stenciled pattern
- Craft knife and cutting mat
- Fabric paint
- Iron
- 14" pillow insert

Make the Pillow Cover

1 On each of the 15" × 11" back pieces, fold over one of the 15" sides ½" and press. Fold over another ½". Press and pin in place. Stitch ¼" from the edge.

2 Place the 15" × 15" front piece right side up on your work surface. Place one of the back pieces right side down with the hemmed edge running across the middle. Place the second back piece right side down with the hemmed edge overlapping the first piece in the middle.

3 Pin around the perimeter making sure to secure every corner and where the three layers meet. Linen is shifty, so lots of pinning keeps the fabric straight as you stitch.

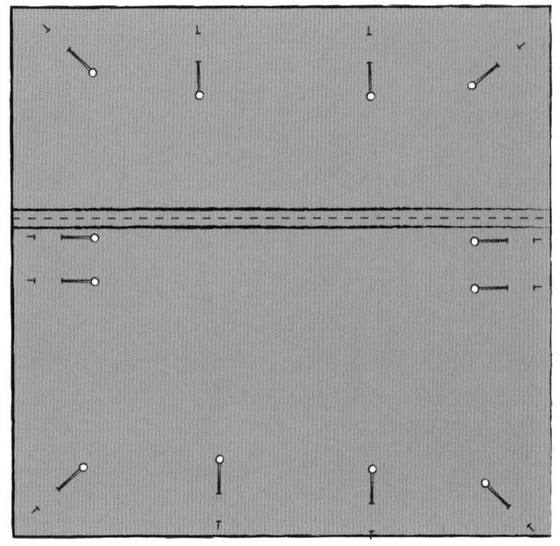
STEP 3

4 Sew around all four sides with a ½" seam allowance. Snip each corner. Go around once more using a zigzag stitch along the edge of the fabric to prevent future fraying.

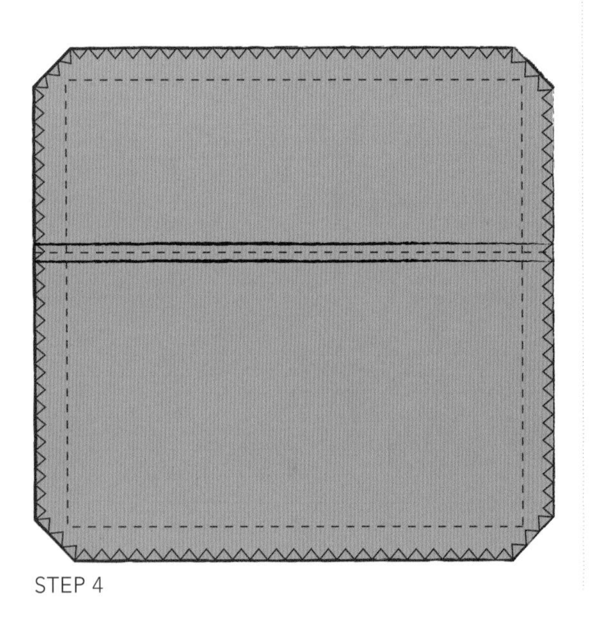
STEP 4

5 Turn the pillow cover inside out. Make sure to poke all the corners into place with a pencil's eraser end.

Stencil

1 Use your craft knife and cutting mat to cut out your equation symbol. Use a ruler to help keep the lines straight. Also use the ruler to find the midpoint of the pillow. Place the stencil center directly onto the pillow midpoint and iron it in place. Remember to insert another piece of freezer paper on the inside of the pillow cover to prevent leaking paint. (For complete information on working with fabric printing, please read Chapter 2.)

NOTE: To make a minus sign, use just one of the bars from the equal sign on page 175.

2 Add paint according to the technique section. Let it dry and then heat set it with an iron.

3 Stuff the cover with a 14" pillow form. Arrange several pillows together to create an environment with both design appeal and learning potential. Consider setting a basket of counting inspiration close by, such as small blocks or smooth stones.

PORTFOLIO

PORTFOLIO

Finished Dimensions: 9½" × 7½"

This fold-over fabric envelope holds and covers your favorite tools; the dimensions given here are perfect for a journal and pens. (I've also provided suggestions for how to create a larger size customized for a laptop or tablet.) This design plays off of two contrasting colors of linen and uses low tech "soft-ware" (a handmade strap) for the closure. The back side is a perfect canvas for a stencil. This small portfolio has its print on the inside flap for a special glimpse every time it's opened.

Prepare the Envelope

1 Make the strap from the 3" × 11" piece of linen. Fold linen in half lengthwise and press with a hot iron. Open and fold each side just to the crease. Fold in half again. The crease is on one side and the folded edges are on the other. Sew a straight stitch along the edge of each side. Set aside.

2 Place all three rectangular layers on top of one another in this order: batting, linen, linen. Linen does not have a right side, unless it's a print. If you are working with a print, make sure that the two pieces of linen are right side to right side on top of the batting.

3 Cut off two top corners to create an envelope V-shape.

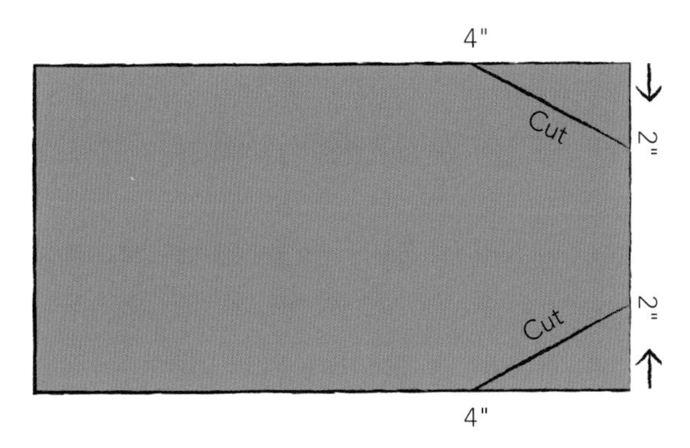

STEP 3

SUPPLIES

- 2 10" × 20" linen rectangles in contrasting colors
- 10" × 20" piece batting
- 3" × 11" linen strip for the strap to match the interior color
- Coordinating thread
- Printed stencil pattern
- Fabric paint and brush
- Craft knife and cutting mat

4 Insert the strap between the two layers of linen 1½" from the bottom. Pin every layer together, making certain that both sides of the strap are placed evenly. Pin around the perimeter of the portfolio.

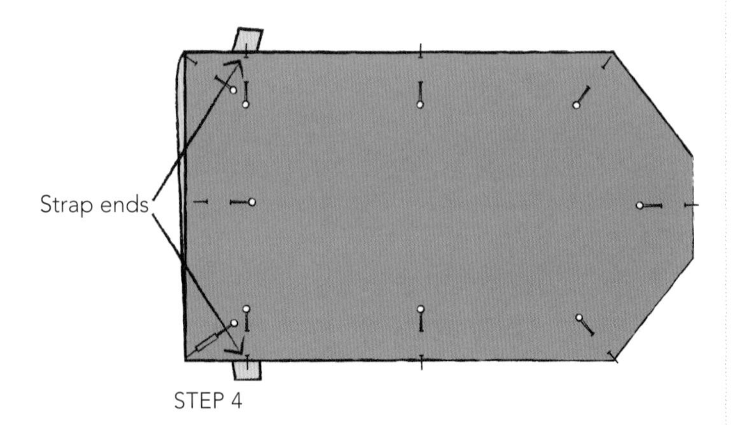

STEP 4

5 Using a ¼" seam allowance, sew around the perimeter leaving 4" open in the bottom center for turning. This opening is opposite to the envelope side. Clip each corner. Clip off excess of any of the strap edges to make them flush with the rest of the portfolio.

6 Turn the piece right side out and gently poke out the corners using the eraser end of a pencil.

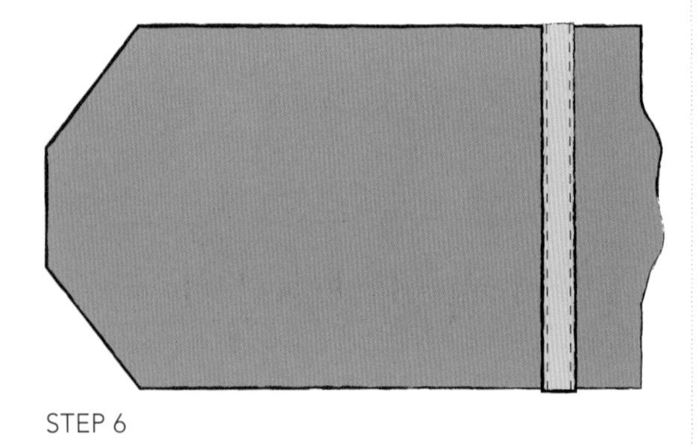

STEP 6

7 Tuck in the open side and pin it closed. Press the whole piece.

8 Edge stitch along the entire bottom making sure to catch the sides of the opening in the seam allowance.

Assemble the Envelope

1 Fold up the bottom 6½" inches. Because the strap can still slip to either side, make sure it is on the chosen outside, not the interior, and then pin in place.

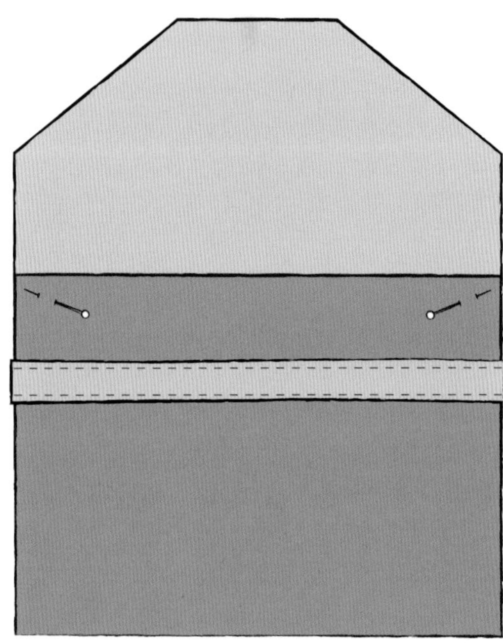

STEP 1

2 Starting on a bottom corner, edge stitch up and around the envelope, excluding the bottom folded side.

3 If you'd like to embellish the portfolio, select a stencil, decide where you want to place it, and follow the instructions in Chapter 2 for printing. Slip in your tool of choice and you're off!

Formula for Creating a Larger Portfolio

If you'd like to make a larger portfolio to cover a specific notebook, laptop, or tablet then use the following suggestions for figuring out the measurements of your supplies and modify the project steps as specified. The example used is a laptop.

1 Find the length of the envelope rectangle by wrapping a measuring tape around a closed laptop widthwise. Jot down that number. Next, figure out how many inches are needed for the fold-over flap by measuring ¾ of the way across the top widthwise. Add those inches to your first measurement. This number is the length of the rectangle.

For example: 19½" + 6" = 25½"

2 Find the width of the rectangle by measuring the height of the computer and doubling it. Add that number to the length of the computer plus 1". For example: ¾" × 2 + 13" + 1" = 15½"

Cut three rectangles 25½" × 15½".

The strap remains the same width regardless of the size of the portfolio. Lengthen it to be as long as the width of the rectangle + 1".

3 Modify Step 3 of the "Prepare the Envelope" section by cutting off the corners to form an envelope V shape where you see fit for your new size.

4 Modify Step 4 of the "Prepare the Envelope" section by pinning the strap 2" from the bottom. Keep the placement the same as the original for smaller tablets.

NOTE: These modifications are recommendations, but customization will involve using your own logic, as well.

REVERSIBLE SUMMER SLING

REVERSIBLE SUMMER SLING

Finished Dimensions: 17" × 32"

Warmer days and the lure of spontaneous adventures call for a handbag with versatility and ease. This sling holds more than just the essentials, and because it's reversible it will perform miraculous transformations to match your mood and wardrobe. Here, one side remains soft and neutral, whereas the other makes a bold statement with high-contrast colors and a printed pocket. The adjustable knot allows for custom sizing and many different carrying options. There are two pockets that easily morph from interior to exterior depending on which way it's worn. There's a lot to this deceptively simple sling!

NOTE: A long skirt or wide pant legs often provides enough yardage for this project. A clever and playful alternative is to create your own 38" × 18" pieces by sewing strips of different colored linen together to create a striped effect. If you want to use yardage, you'll need 1⅜ yards of fabric for the interior and 1⅜ yards fabric for the exterior.

SUPPLIES

- 2 38" × 18" pieces of linen for exterior
- 2 38" × 18" pieces of linen for interior
- 2 11" × 10" pieces of linen
- 2 8"-diameter linen circles
- 2 buttons
- Coordinating thread
- 4" twill tape or rug binding tape
- Stencil pattern
- Ruler
- Tailor's chalk
- Fabric paint and brush
- Craft knife and cutting mat

Cut the Linen Pieces

1 Cut out the template from page 183. Make sure to enlarge it as directed on the template.

2 Fold one of the 38" × 18" pieces of linen for the interior in half lengthwise. Measure 6" from the bottom. Place the template on the fold. Pin in place.

3 Using a ruler and tailor's chalk sketch the rest of the measurements onto the fabric using the diagram. Cut along the chalk lines and use this first piece as the pattern for the other interior piece and the two exterior pieces that make up the body of the bag. Cut out two 8" circles for the bottoms and two 11" × 10" pieces for the pockets. (See Chapter 1 for information on creating a circle template.)

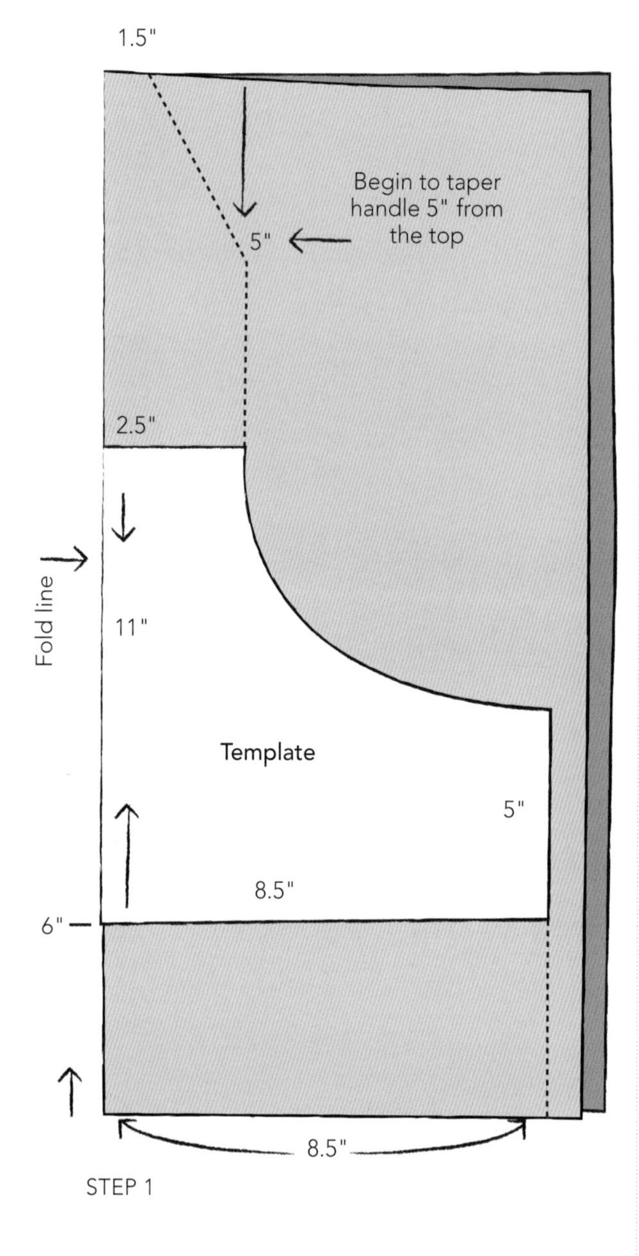

Assemble the Interior

1 Lay the two interior pieces right sides together. The curve will be in the center and the sides will measure 11". Sew one of these sides with a ½" seam. Press the seam allowance open.

2 Make a pocket from the 11" × 10" rectangle. Create the top hem by folding a 10" side over ½". Press the fold and fold over ½" again. Press. Topstitch with a ⅜" seam allowance.

3 For each 11" side fold over ¼" and press. Fold over ¼" and press again.

4 Center the pocket piece directly over the 11" side seam on the right side of the just-sewn bag. The hemmed edge of the pocket is up and the bottom edge is left untouched and flush with the bottom of the bag. Pin in place.

5 Optional loop for keys, etc.: Fold the twill tape or rug binding tape in half and insert the raw edges along the side of the pocket a couple of inches from the top.

6 Stitch the pocket in place with two parallel seams. Backstitch at the top of the pocket several times and over the twill tape each time for extra reinforcing on stress points.

7 Lay the interior bag right sides together and sew the other 11" side, leaving a 4" hole open for turning when the exterior and interior are put together.

8 Baste stitch the bottom opening using a ¼" seam and gather the bottom to fit the 8" circle (see the gathering instructions in Chapter 1). Pull the thread and push the fabric until it is evenly dispersed and the bottom opening measures 12" when placed flat along a ruler. Pin the 8" interior circle to the bottom. Ease it into place so that there aren't any creases on the circle side. Switch your stitch length back to a standard length and sew the bottom with a ½" seam allowance.

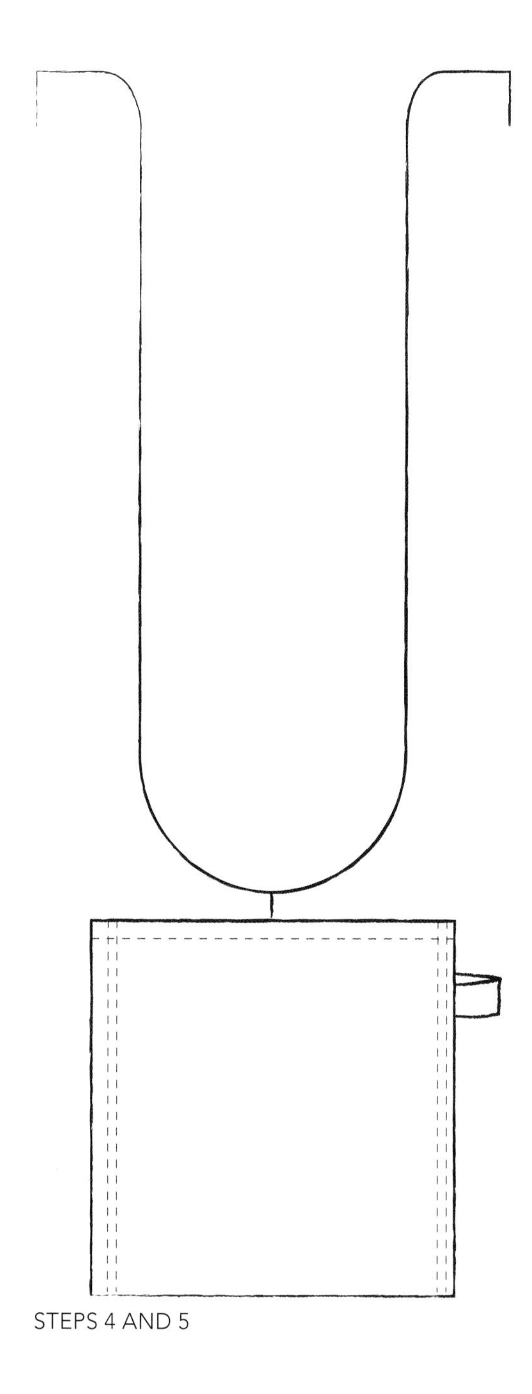

STEPS 4 AND 5

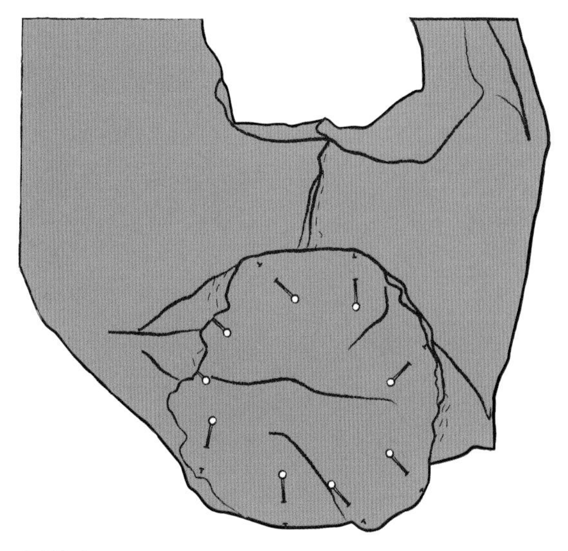

STEP 8

Assemble the Exterior

1 Follow the exact same steps as you did for the interior, but don't leave a turning hole on one side as described in Step 7. Also topstitch the side seams and bottom circle for an extra "finished" look. Remember to topstitch before adding the pocket! The twill tape loop is optional on the exterior's pocket.

2 From the exterior fabric, create a button loop with a 1" × 8" strip of linen. Fold the strip in half and press to make a crease down the middle of the strip. Open the strip and fold in the long edges so they meet at the crease. Fold once more and press. Working with such a narrow strip takes patience. Stitch down one side; because the strip is so skinny the seam will essentially be in the middle. Fold the strip in half lengthwise and lay the two short ends side by side. Insert a pin 2" from the end. Sew both ends with a button stitch or large, tight zigzag stitch. Stop at the pin.

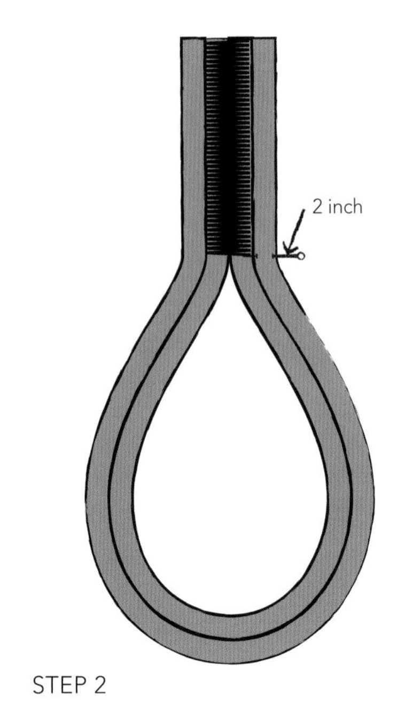

STEP 2

3 Insert the bag exterior with right side out into the bag interior with right side in so the two right sides are facing. The pockets should be on the same side. Sandwich the button loop between both bags and pin it to the seam opposite from the pockets. The loop side should be tucked down into the bags, and the ends should be up along the top edge. Make sure all four side seams are lined up and pin the entire perimeter of the bag together.

4 Stitch around the entire bag with a ½" seam allowance.

5 Turn the bag through the 4" hole you left in the interior on the side seam and poke out the handles. Press the entire bag. Add buttons to each pocket, using the loop to aid in correct placement. Hand-stitch the hole through which you turned the bag.

6 Cut and transfer stencils to one or both pockets and print according to the stencil techniques chapter. This bag is ready for any summer adventure!

CHAPTER 4

BURLAP

Woven jute yarn creates a breathable loose weave that's incredibly durable and naturally earth friendly. Burlap is a utilitarian fabric that is commonly used for transporting goods from tree saplings to coffee beans and potatoes. In today's fast-paced coffee culture, discarded coffee sacks are piling up waiting for reuse.

History

Jute originated in India, where it thrives during the monsoon season. This plant fiber was traditionally grown for paper and rope, but in the 18th century it was discovered by English traders. They brought it home and soon learned to spin it into yarn, which was in turn woven into burlap cloth. Burlap mills sprung up across India when a method for weaving a superior cloth was discovered. In Europe burlap is more commonly referred to as Hessian, named after the soldiers from the German state of Hesse who wore uniforms constructed out of it. This drab and humble cloth is sought out for its weather resistance, strength, and breathability, and over the centuries it has remained the utility fabric of choice in many industries.

Sourcing

Green coffee beans are delivered to roasters in burlap sacks of varied weave. The most desirable for sewing are the sacks of finer weave and softer texture. Avoid the loosely woven, coarse varieties. Each sack comes in a standard size with similar construction, but varied lettering details the country of origin and often the farm the beans were grown on. The graphics can range from simple to elaborate typography, sometimes incorporating colorful pieces of art printed directly onto each sack.

Deconstruction

- Open all of the seams to determine how much usable fabric is available. Some sacks have internal seams; others have an exposed braided binding. Use sharp scissors to cut through the stitching of any internal seams and simply slice off the braided binding. You can save these braided bindings for future projects that need handles and straps.
- Because pitchforks are often used to lift heavy sacks, random holes are a common issue. You can mend many of the holes by adjusting the jute threads. Pull them into place with your fingers or a crochet hook. If the strands of jute have actually been cut, then avoid using that section of the sack as the hole may widen.
- When the burlap is ready to work with, determine the section of the sack that you will cut for your project. Although you can use shears, a rotary blade, cutting mat, and ruler are very helpful for this step. When using a cutting mat, line up the weave as close to the mat's grid as possible. Burlap is shifty; try not to move it out of place as you cut. Weights are helpful. Cans of soup or beans make wonderful improvised weights to hold burlap in place. In addition, creating a paper window enhances your ability to visualize the graphics and their placement. Use a paper bag or newspaper. Outline the dimensions of your project in the center of the paper and cut them out. Set that piece aside. Hold the paper with the cut-out hole over the sack and move it around until you find the desired graphics.

Tips

- Search for clean and gently blemished sacks. Avoid washing machines and dryers, which have the potential to erase graphics and turn burlap into a frayed mess. Instead, air the sacks on a clothesline and spot clean. If you must wash them, iron the graphics in an attempt to heat set them first. Then, proceed to hand wash them in cold water. Hang the sacks to dry in the sun. Burlap does not smell pleasant when it's wet, but fresh air and heat from the sun or a wood stove will dissipate odors.
- Take advantage of burlap's loose weave for cutting straight lines. Pull a thread of jute from one end in the direction that you'd like to cut. For example, for a horizontal cut, pull out a horizontal thread from either side to leave a straight and clear path to guide in cutting. Because the graphics on sacks have a tendency to be printed askew, following the weave of the burlap may result in the print being lopsided. If this is the case, I always cut with the straight line following the graphics rather than the weave.
- Although I love to use up my scraps, jute/burlap is made from plant matter . . . you can compost the pieces you don't save!

Environmental Impact

Burlap is considered one of the greener materials because it is made from a renewable plant source, jute, which is a rain-fed crop that needs little in the way of fertilizer or pesticides to thrive. Burlap is also biodegradable, but any material that has potential to fill up landfills is suitable for rescue.

ONION AND GARLIC SACKS

ONION AND GARLIC SACKS

Finished Dimensions: garlic sack—6½" × 7½" • onion sack—9½" × 9½"

Bulbs and roots need to be kept in a cool, ventilated spot for optimum freshness. Burlap's loose weave is utilized to create the best storage ever for garlic and onions. These sacks feature handy jute loops for hanging, which frees up valuable kitchen counter space. A folk art-inspired print labels each sack. Alternatively, you can stencil the word "garlic" or "onion" across the front in any language or font desired.

SUPPLIES

- 8" × 17" piece of burlap for the garlic sack
- 11" × 22" piece of burlap for the onion sack
- 4 6" lengths of jute twine
- Printed freezer paper stencil
- Craft knife and cutting mat
- Black fabric paint and brush
- Thread

Make the Sacks

1 Fold one piece of your burlap in half lengthwise and pin the sides together.

2 Sew each side with a ½" seam allowance. Trim the seam allowance ever so slightly; you just want to trim enough to make sure each side is even with another. Use a zigzag stitch along the edge to contain the fray.

3 Hem the opening. Fold over the edges of the opening ¾" and press. Repeat by folding over ¾" and pressing once more.

4 To make your jute loops, fold each length of jute in half. Insert the loose ends under the folded hem at the sack opening 1" away from each side seam. Keeping the loop ends tucked under, fold the loops up against the hem and pin them in place. The result is that each sack will have two loops on the back side that extend approximately (but evenly to one another) 1" above the hemmed opening.

5 Sew around the bottom edge of the fold, making sure to backstitch over each loop. Edge stitch a second time at the top of the hem. This gives each sack a parallel seam at the top that securely holds the loops and provides a nice structure to the opening while the sack is hanging.

STEP 4

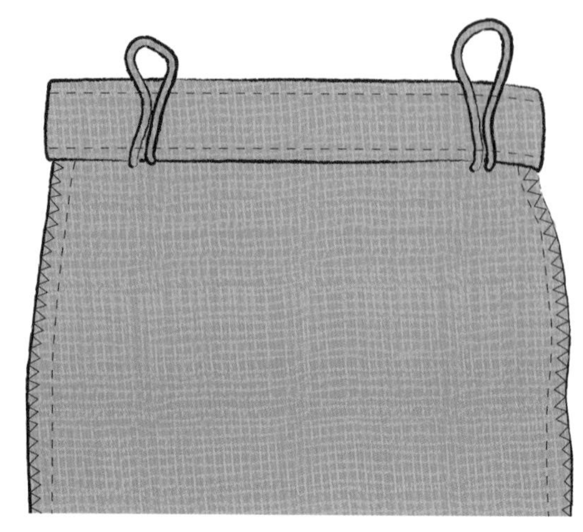

STEP 5

6 Turn the sack right side out and gently poke out the corners at the bottom of the sack. Take care with the burlap's loose weave; you don't want to poke too forcefully.

7 Repeat the process in Steps 1 through 6 with your other piece of burlap.

Stencil the Motifs

1 Cut out the stencils on page 177. Make sure to label each piece before you begin cutting and refer to Chapter 3 for inserting *islands*.

2 Stenciling on burlap requires extra care when adhering paper to the fabric. Press thoughtfully and firmly with a hot iron.

3 Paint the design and wait until it's dry to the touch.

4 Remove the stencil and heat set it.

5 Hang your sacks in your kitchen!

LOG CARRIER

LOG CARRIER

Finished Dimensions: Large carrier—20" × 39" • Mini carrier—15½" × 39"

A steady supply of fuel is the key to a cozy home. When heating with wood, this sling makes the job of hauling logs from the pile a simple task. It sews up quickly by utilizing a coffee sack in its original form with only slight alterations. Attaching sturdy jute upholstery webbing for the handle holders ensures that this carrier can live up to its rugged good looks. Slip in handles made from foraged branches, recycled broom sticks, or readily available dowels. Measurements for a smaller size are included so that even the littlest of helpers can be involved. Additionally, tying the handles together with a loop of jute transforms this sling into a newspaper tote for storing and transporting your paper to the recycling bin during the warmer months.

SUPPLIES

Large Log Carrier
- 2 21" × 35" pieces of burlap
- 4 17" × 4" pieces of upholstery jute webbing
- 2 19" strong branches, a broom stick, or thick dowels

Mini Log Carrier
- 2 17" × 27" pieces of burlap
- 4 13" × 4" pieces of upholstery jute webbing
- 2 15" strong branches, a broom stick, or thick dowels

Thread

Cutting mat (optional)

Rotary cutter (optional)

Make Sling

1 Cut off the top, bottom, and both sides of a coffee sack to create two 21" × 35" rectangles. You can cut both pieces simultaneously by laying the sack flat on a cutting surface and using a rotary cutter.

2 Place each layer right side to right side and sew around the perimeter ½" from the edge. Leave an 8" opening on one of the long sides for turning.

3 Turn the piece right side out and pin closed the opening. Press with a hot iron. Edge stitch around the entire bag.

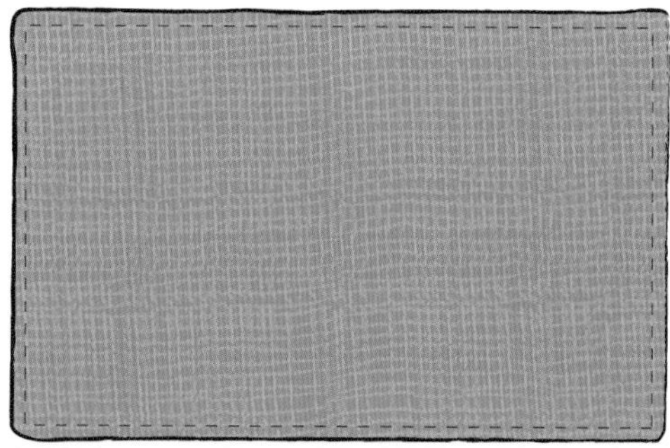

STEP 3

Make Handle Holders

1 Fold under each raw edge of the webbing ½" and sew in place with two parallel seams.

2 Fold the webbing in half lengthwise to make a crease. Fit the edge of the sack into the crease of the webbing and sandwich 1" of the top of the sack along the bottom of the webbing. Pin the webbing in place. Repeat this on the other three corners.

3 Attach each holder at the bottom edge of the webbing directly to the sack. Begin at the folded side and sew toward the middle of the sling.

4 Sew closed the top of only one holder from each side of the sling. Backstitch at least twice at the end of the seams that are on the top of the webbing at the midpoint of the sling. These will be the stress points when you carry a heavy load of logs.

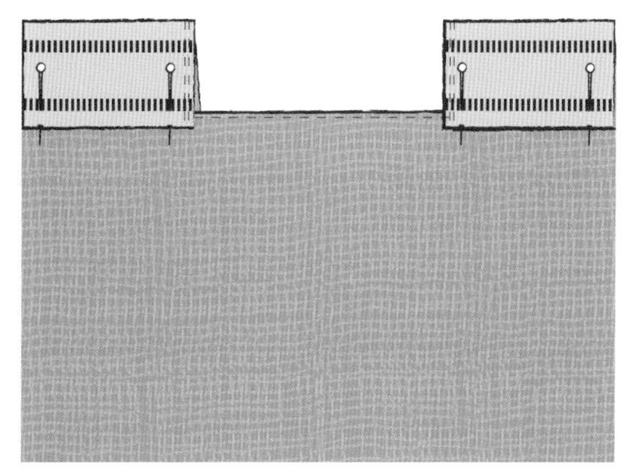

STEP 2

5 Slide in your handles. Pin closed the tops of the two open sides of the holder and sew the handle in place in the same fashion as the other holder tops. Remember to backstitch at least twice at the midpoint of the sling.

6 Carry wood!

INSPIRATION BOARD

INSPIRATION BOARD

Finished Dimensions: 17" × 23"

Cover an everyday bulletin board with a coffee sack and a few assorted textile elements to create either a visual home for inspiration or a unique way to stay organized. Each board is as distinct as the found materials it is made of. These basic instructions can be used for any size bulletin board. Create a close replica or make something perfectly suited to your needs. Here you'll find one that organizes a sewing space and another that gathers bits for inspiration.

Measure and Cut the Burlap

1 Take the bulletin board's measurements and determine which orientation (horizontal or vertical) you want to use. Add at least 3" to both the height and width of the board.

2 Use your measurements to determine what section of the coffee sack you are going to use. Pay careful attention to graphics on the sack that might be interesting to highlight.

3 Cut the coffee sack to the required height and width.

Make the Pockets

1 Decide where on the board you want to add pockets and determine how large they should be. To these measurements, add 1" to the width. Double the length and add 1".

2 Cut the linen to the measurements you determined in Step 1.

3 Fold the linen piece in half lengthwise. Sew around the perimeter of the three open edges, leaving an opening opposite the folded edge for turning the piece in the next step.

4 Clip the corners and turn the linen right side out. Fold in the edges of the opening. Pin the opening closed and press the linen. The side with the opening will be the bottom of the pocket.

5 Sew a finishing hem on the folded side/top ¼" from the edge.

6 Stencil desired words or letters onto the pocket or add an embellishment, such as lace or ribbons. The sample has a vintage circular piece sewn to the main pocket as additional storage.

SUPPLIES

- Coffee sack
- Linen scraps or linen pockets removed from clothing, lace, doilies
- Jute webbing
- Cork board with wooden frame
- Textile paints
- Stencils
- Thumbtacks
- Staple gun and staples
- Cotton rug binding tape (enough to cover the entire perimeter of the board)
- Glue gun and glue sticks
- Picture hanging hardware

Arrange Board Elements

1 Place your cut burlap on top of the board so that you can arrange your pockets and other components. Pin each item in place. For example, you can add strips of elastic or rug binding tape for holding pens and rulers. (Make sure to fold under the ends and pin them in place.) Consider using little bits of lace for mini pockets to hold memos and other assorted items. You can hem the edges of a section of upholstery jute and then fold it in half to create a sturdy holster for scissors and other heavy objects.

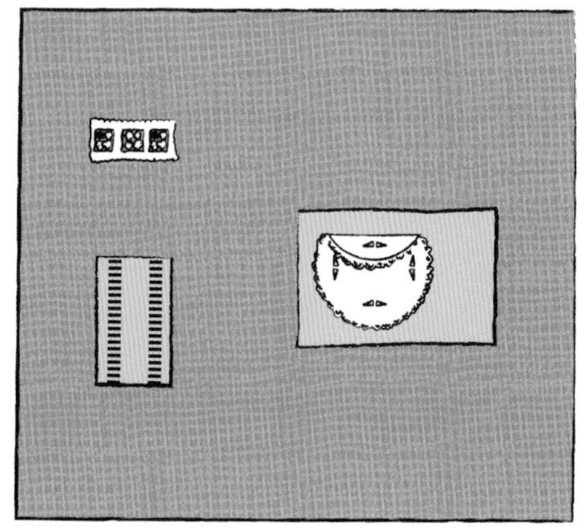

STEP 1

2 Sew each accessory in place on the burlap, making sure to keep the top of the pockets open. Backstitch several times at the top of each side where the pockets will have the most stress.

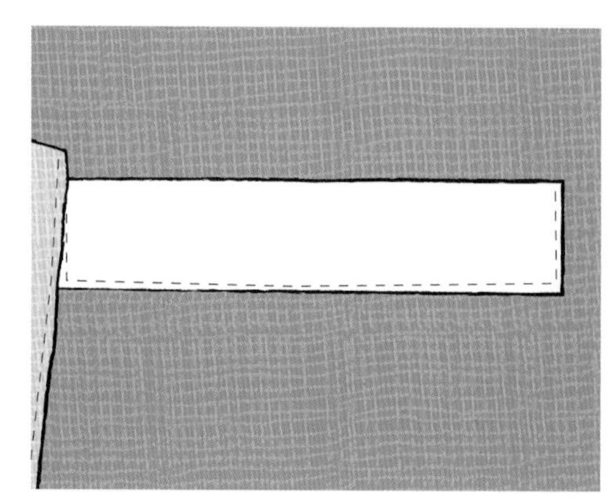

STEP 2

3 After you have attached all the accessories, return the burlap to the board. Gently smooth it out with a little stretch in each direction. Place thumbtacks strategically around the sides to keep everything secure. Check to make sure the graphics on the burlap have not stretched in the wrong direction. If all seems in order for the final product, turn the board face down on your work surface.

Stapling the Burlap to the Board

1 Fold the burlap over the top edge of the board and apply a few staples along the back close to the edge of the frame. After you've added these staples, rotate the board 180° and do the same thing along the bottom edge. Rotate the board 90° and staple a few sections on the left side and then rotate again to staple the right side. Turn the board over periodically to check your work. Make sure to neatly tuck in the corners. Continue this method of rotating and stapling until you have approximately one staple per inch around the entire frame.

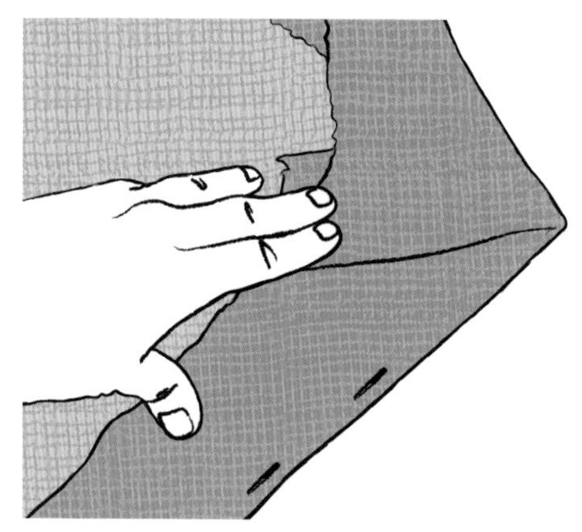

STEP 1

2 When the board is complete, cut off the excess burlap.

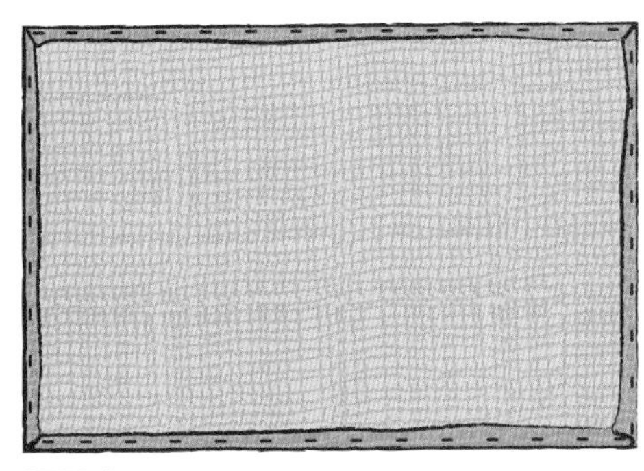
STEP 2

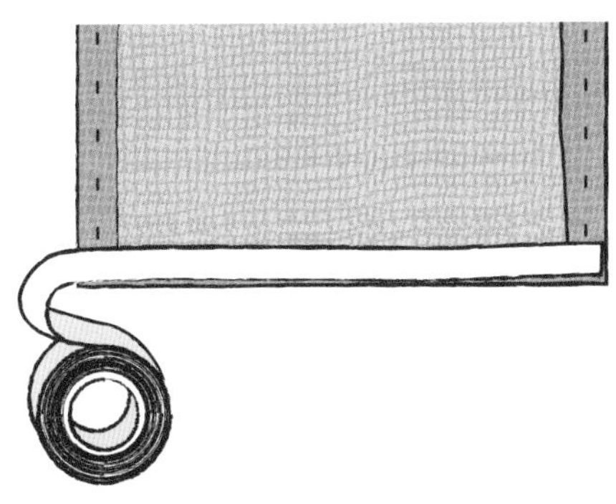
STEP 3

3 To protect your wall from the numerous staples, use the rug binding tape to cover the staples. Using a hot glue gun, attach a strip of rug binding tape along the right and left sides of the board. Cut two strips that are slightly longer than the length of your top and bottom sides. Fold under the ends of the strips for a tidy look and use the hot glue gun to apply the strips to the top and bottom edges of the board.

4 Add the picture hanging hardware by going straight through the jute and webbing and into the bulletin board frame. You might need to use a hammer with a nail to get the screw holes started through so many layers.

5 Your board is ready to hang and keep you organized!

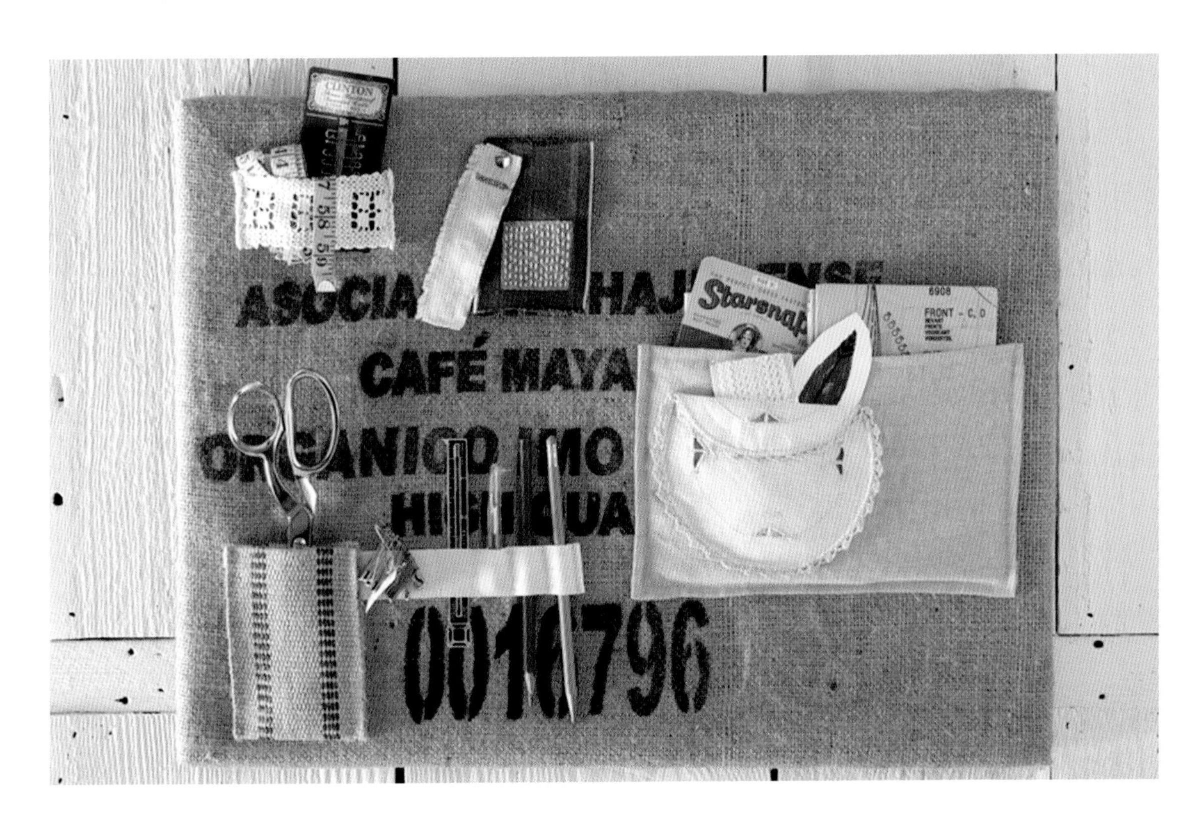

Variation

A wonderful alternative to sewing on pockets is to cut the ready-made pockets from linen clothing and add them to an already covered burlap board. This version allows for improvisation and constant rearranging, which is very desirable for a gathering of inspiration—such as this board with the theme of flight. How do you do it? Trim around the edges of each pocket carefully. Tack them in place for holding treasures and collections. That's it! Easy and versatile.

BURLAP BIN

Dwellings
CATSKILLS COUNTRY
THE WAY WE LIVE
COFFEE
GUATEMALA
ORGANIC
CLEAN
PRODUCT
COFFEE
GUATEMALA
2008-2009

BURLAP BIN

Finished Dimensions: Small bin—7" × 7" • Large bin—11" × 11"

These storage bins will corral toys, books, and art supplies with style and ease. Create a center handle slot so you can pull the bin off a shelf, or insert a handle on each side for convenient carrying. They're a fantastic alternative to yesterday's plastic tubs, and the bold typography of salvaged coffee sacks makes these worth displaying. These cubed bins can be sized to fit exactly where you need them most. In addition, they conveniently nest together or fold flat to take up minimal space when they're not in use. But when will that really happen? You'll be making them in multiples for every room in the house!

SUPPLIES

- 5 squares of burlap (8" × 8" for a small bin; 12" × 12" for a large bin)
- 5 squares of liner fabric in cotton or heavy linen, cut to the same dimensions as the burlap
- 5 squares of batting cut to the same dimensions as the burlap
- 2 rectangles of liner fabric for each handle slot (4" × 8" for a small bin; 4" × 12" for a large bin)
- Extra sewing machine needle (just in case); a universal needle works well, but some machines might benefit from using a denim needle with heavy burlap
- Needle and thread for basting
- Seam ripper
- Ruler
- Pencil
- Scissors
- 4 clothespins

NOTE: One half of a coffee sack is enough to make one small bin. The larger size requires a whole sack. Also, the supplies listed here will make one burlap bin. If you're making a set of bins, make sure to increase the quantity of supplies according to the number of bins you want to have.

Create the Handle Slots

1 Lay a liner square right side up on top of a batting square. Pin one *rectangle* of liner fabric wrong side up for the handle slot to the top portion of the right side of a liner square. Pin one *rectangle* of liner fabric to the top portion of the right side of a burlap square. Use a ruler and pencil to draw a 1" × 4" rectangle 1½" from the top and 2" from the right and left sides. Draw a dividing line down the center of the slot lengthwise and a triangle from the center line to the box's corners. Do this for both the burlap and liner squares.

2 Beginning with the liner square, stitch around the perimeter of the drawn rectangle. Remember to lock stitches at both ends.

3 Snip through the dividing line just up to the point of the triangle and then cut along the angled lines of the triangle. Take care not to snip too close to the stitches.

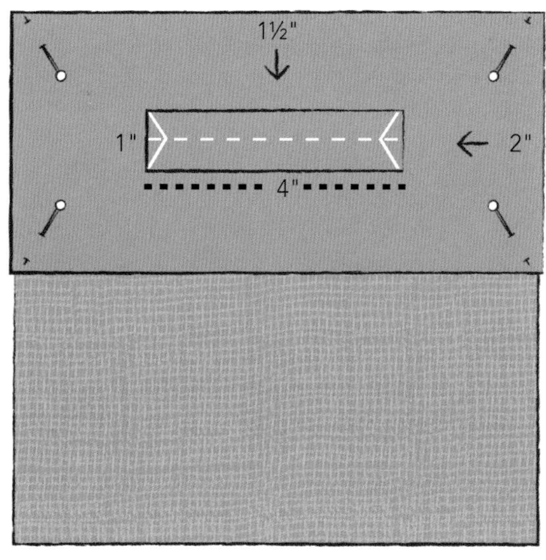

STEP 1

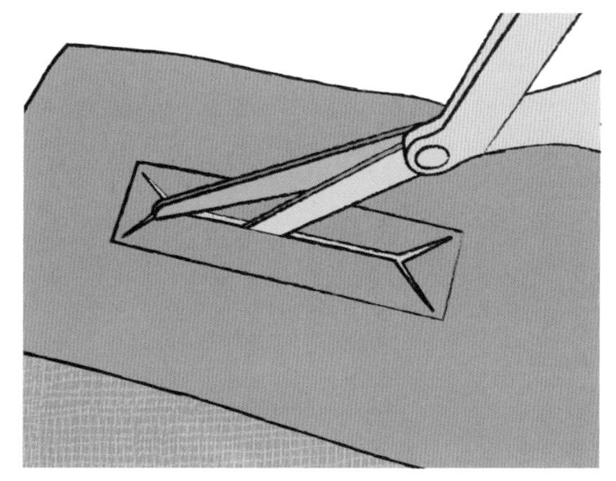
STEP 3

4 Remove the pins and gently pull the entire rectangle of fabric through the slot. Smooth it out on the other side.

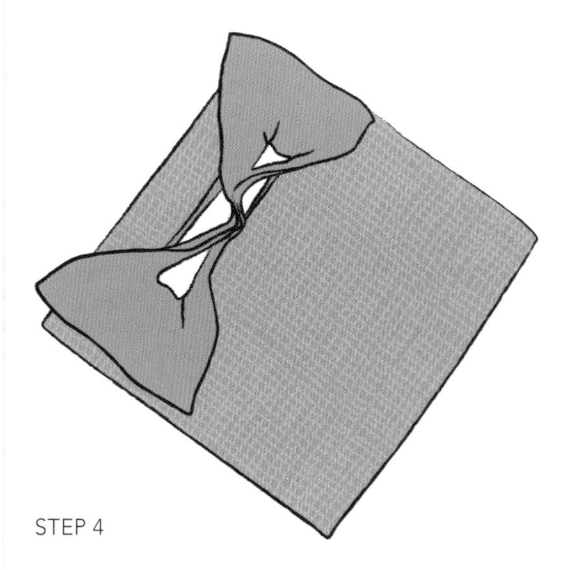
STEP 4

5 Finger press the corners until it's nice and square. Press in place (with an iron this time). Repeat these steps with the burlap square so that there are two squares with matching slots.

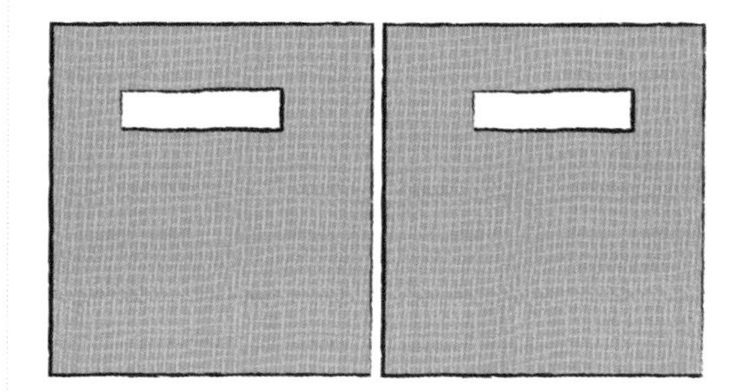

6 Repeat these steps if you are making a two-slotted bin.

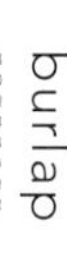

Assemble the Bin

1 Pin two burlap squares together with right sides facing and sew down one side with a ¼" seam. Continue adding squares until all four sides have been attached to create a bottomless cube. Make sure the slots are positioned correctly (that is, at the top and opposite from each other if there are two).

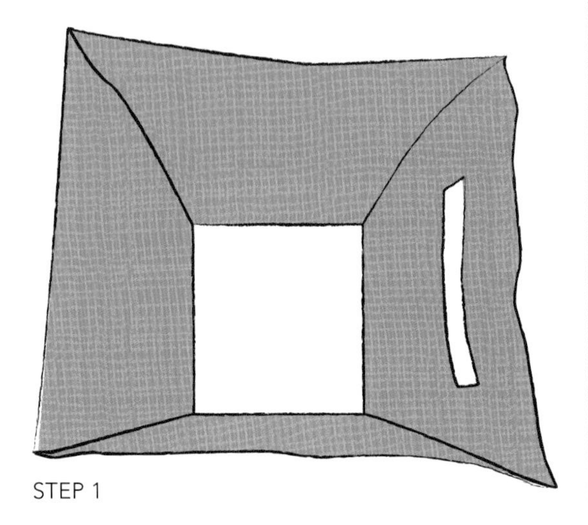

STEP 1

2 Sew along the seam allowance of each side with a zigzag stitch to enclose the frayed loose edges of the burlap and secure this loose weave.

3 Pin the fifth burlap square right side up to the bottom of the open cube, matching all four corners. Attach with a ¼" seam. Reinforce with a zigzag stitch around the edges just as you did for the sides.

4 Turn the cube right side out and press all seams with an iron.

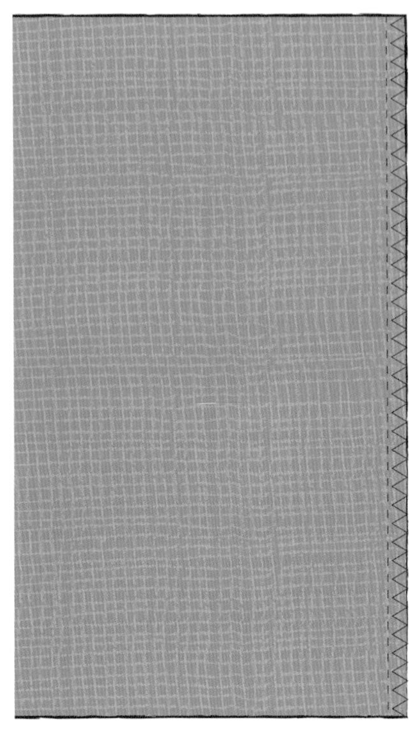

STEP 2

5 Match all liner squares with a piece of batting to their wrong side. With right sides facing, sew all four batting-backed liner squares together with a ¼" seam. Pin the bottom square (with batting) to the cube and sew with a ½" seam allowance. Trim all excess seam allowances.

6 Insert the burlap bin into the liner right side to right side. Line up all of the corners and the slots. Pin in place. Sew around the perimeter of the top with a ¼" seam allowance leaving a 6" gap for turning. Remove the pins and gently pull the liner through the gap and then pull the burlap through with extra care. Poke out the corners and push the liner into place.

STEP 6

7 Pin the gap shut and press the entire perimeter. Match the slots of the exterior and the liner and pin them in place. Edge stitch around the entire perimeter of the bag, sealing shut the gap. Go slowly over the corners, as they are thick.

Finish the Slots

1 Baste the two layers of the slot together with a whip stitch around the opening.

2 Top stitch around the slot on the burlap side. Take care to keep the lines of the rectangle straight and perpendicular to one another.

3 Remove the basting threads with a seam ripper. Press once more and block overnight with a clothespin at each corner. In the morning the bin will be ready for filling!

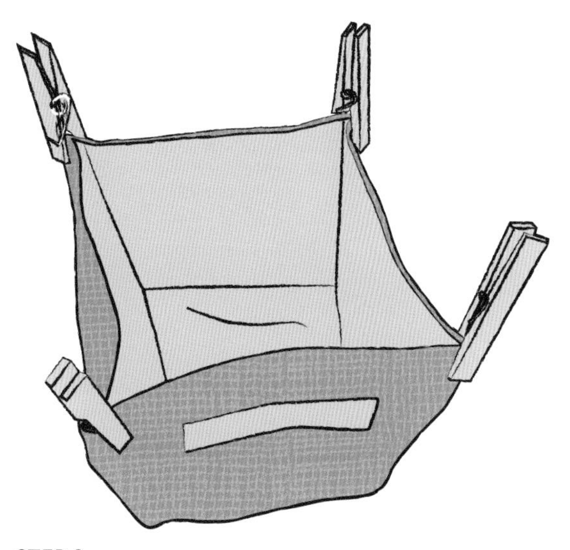

STEP 3

Note on Handles for Increased Sizes

To make different sized bins, simply increase or decrease the square size. Make sure to keep this in mind when cutting the rectangle of liner fabric for the handle slot. It will remain 4" on one side. The other measurement is determined by how many inches your new square is. For instance, the large bin shown is made from 12" squares. The liner fabric for creating the handle slot is 4" × 12". Whatever the size of the new bin, the slot itself is always placed in the top center. The slot itself can remain the same size for larger bins, and continue to be positioned 1½" from the top edge.

To add a handle slot to both sides, repeat the handle slot instructions for another side and remember to position the handle slots opposite from another when sewing together the four sides of a bin.

Coffee Sack Hack

Several years ago, I was designing the autumn window display for a children's resale shop. I was on the look-out for an interesting and recycled backdrop, so I called the roasting headquarters of our local coffee shop in the hope that they had some leftover coffee bean sacks. They were thrilled to have me take some off their hands, and I was pleased to discover how gorgeous they were. Beautiful prints and bold typography graced each one. I selected a few for the store window and took a couple home. One of them had my name on it, literally, and I hung it on my studio wall right next to a bulletin board. The sack was only a little bit larger than the board, and seeing them side by side inspired me to cover the board with the burlap. I instantly fell in love with this rustic and repurposed material.

Next, I wanted a burlap handbag so that I could carry those big black printed letters with me everywhere. I was hesitant to run such thick fibers through my sewing machine, but couldn't stop myself. The first sewing attempt with a coffee sack was a surprising success. Simultaneously, the bulletin board, which I had shared on my blog, was soaring across the blogosphere from one big design site to another. I knew I was on to something, and I ran to the coffee roasters for more sacks. This time, I asked the burlap what it wanted to be. Its original use for holding and storing things inspired me to duplicate those same functions for home use. Burlap bins were born!

I opened an online shop and was shocked at how fast they flew off the shelves. My passion for rescuing and reinventing this humble material was matched by the enthusiasm of everyone who saw them. For months I perfected and sewed bin after bin. Wholesale requests poured in, big box stores contacted me. However, the burlap bin business was taking its toll. I hired an assistant, but I knew that I'd never be able to make enough to rescue all of the sacks stacking up in warehouses around the world. I decided to sell my original pattern and encourage others to salvage sacks in their own communities. It was a turning point. I discovered that I enjoyed sharing the process of rescuing and reinventing materials as much, and even more, than my love for burlap. Patterns and workshops were the perfect new direction for my journey with rescued materials. ■

CHAPTER 5

JERSEY

Just about everyone has owned at least one t-shirt. They are the garment equivalent to comfort food and are synonymous with contemporary casual wear. Soft and comfortable, t-shirts are the most common use of the stretch knit fabric, jersey. They come in every color of the rainbow and offer abundant inspiration for transformation.

History

T-shirts evolved from 19th century union suits that were cropped in half for comfort by miners and dockworkers. The classic, pull-on and button-free white t-shirt first gained popularity when the U.S. Navy issued them as undershirts during the Spanish-American War. By the time the Great Depression hit, t-shirts were regularly worn for chores and labor, but were not recognized as acceptable attire until Marlon Brando popularized them in *A Streetcar Named Desire*. The 1960s revolutionized the wearing of t-shirts as more than fashion statements; they became canvases for political and artistic expression featuring tie-dye and silkscreen printing. Corporations and concert promoters quickly recognized their potential as walking advertisements. The t-shirt printing business was born.

Sourcing

Besides the stack of old t-shirts most of us have in the back of our closets, they are available in abundance at used clothing stores. To get the most fabric out of each shirt, look for XL or larger in the men's section. Shirts with minimal graphics offer the most potential for personalization. Check labels for 100% cotton and let your hand determine the weight and softness of each shirt. Heavy-weight cotton jersey is recommended for all projects in this chapter.

Deconstructing

- Most t-shirts have a similar anatomy. The bottom hem has a double row of stitches and a narrow channel that you can utilize for an assortment of projects that call for a finished edge or for threading elastic and drawstrings. Remove this channel carefully by cutting right along the top or middle of the double seams. The Blossom Band features a bottom hem channel as a base for embellishing.
- Cut off sleeves, following the contour of the seam from under the armpit to the shoulder. You can use them as headbands and kerchiefs by simply slipping them over your head.
- Remove the neckline channel. Next, cut along a side seam to open up the shirt for use. Some t-shirts are constructed as a tube and don't have any side seams. These offer a long seamless piece of jersey yardage when you slit them up one side.

Tips

- Use a jersey machine needle that has a ballpoint tip to punch through the weave of the fabric rather than cutting it and creating holes.

- Stitch with a zigzag, mock overlock, or longer stitch on jersey in areas that will get a lot of stretching. Test swatches of fabric to make sure that the stitches hold when gently pulled. Experiment.
- Gently guide jersey through your sewing machine. Any pulling or tugging causes unwanted stretching and ripples seams, especially if the material is light weight.
- Lettuce ruffle edging adds a sweet and feminine finishing to the raw edges of jersey. Set your sewing machine to a tight zigzag, essentially a satin stitch. Sew along a raw edge and stretch the fabric in both directions as you go. Take care to still let your machine feed the fabric and don't pull it through.
- Raw edges curl but don't unravel.

Environmental Impact

Huge! Many people are not aware of the toxic journey a seemingly innocent t-shirt takes before arriving in the dresser drawer. Cotton production includes massive use of the most harmful insecticides and synthetic fertilizers. One-third of a pound of poisons are used per shirt. Heavy chemicals, including harsh petroleum scours, ammonia, and formaldehyde (to name a few) continue to be used throughout the manufacturing process. It's unfortunate that even after all of this damage, the t-shirt's journey often ends in a landfill because t-shirts are frequently viewed as disposable. What can be done?

- Educate yourself and those around you so that you can make choices that you feel good about.
- Seek out used t-shirts for your wardrobe.
- Encourage companies to find alternatives to promotional t-shirts, which are the most commonly discarded.
- Purchase organic cotton t-shirts.
- Reinvent using discarded t-shirts!

PILLOW PAL

PILLOW PAL

Finished dimensions: elephant—11" × 12" • robot—11" × 14"

Is it a stuffed toy, a pillow, or a pajama bag? It's all three! Made from a soft and cuddly t-shirt, this pillow comes in the shape of either a tired baby elephant or a sleepy robot. A hidden back pocket holds pajamas, a favorite bedtime story, or secret treasures. A Pillow Pal makes a wonderful hand-made gift and a perfect travel accessory for a lucky child. Each one triples as storage, comfort, and play.

Print the Pillow

1 Transfer chosen stencil to freezer paper and cut with a craft knife. Refer to Chapter 2 for more details.

2 Place the stencil in the top center of the t-shirt and iron all the pieces in place. Slip another piece of freezer paper in between the t-shirt layers to prevent the paint from bleeding through.

3 Use a sleeve to test how your paint color will appear on the t-shirt.

4 Apply fabric paint and let it completely dry before peeling off the stencil pieces. Remove the extra freezer paper from inside the shirt and heat set the paint.

Assemble the Pillow

1 Draw around the new print with chalk leaving a 2" margin. Smooth out both layers of the shirt and make sure there aren't any wrinkles and creases on the back side. Cut directly through both layers with a rotary cutter. If you only have scissors, make sure to securely pin the front and back together before cutting. Set aside.

2 Open up the remaining part of the t-shirt by cutting along a side seam. Place the wrong side up with the bottom hem positioned at the top. Place the two layers of the cut-out pillow on top of the hem. The hem should reach ¾ of the way up the back of the pillow. Pin all three layers in place and cut out the bottom layer using the top layers as a template.

SUPPLIES

- T-shirt with minimal or no graphics
- Fabric paint
- Stencil
- Freezer paper
- Craft knife
- Stuffing
- Tailor's chalk
- Rotary cutter and cutting mat or scissors
- Pins

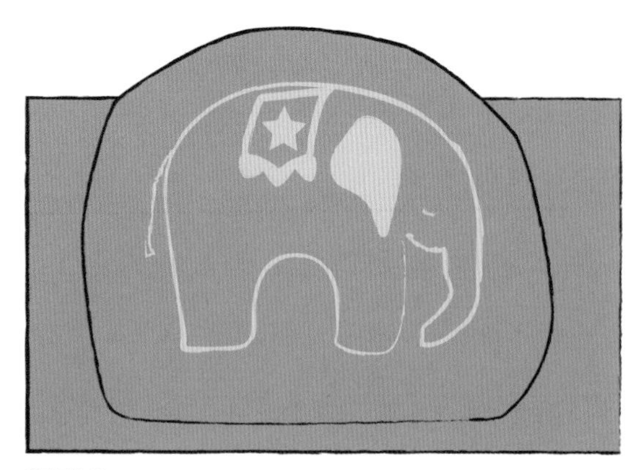
STEP 2

NOTE: Laying the pieces on the grid of a cutting mat can help you make sure that the hem is straight.

3 Take the stenciled top off. Flip over the two back sides so that they are both facing right side up. Place the stenciled side down on top of them. Pin the three layers together. Add an optional loop by cutting 5" of the bottom hem from the t-shirt. Fold the strip in half and insert the folded side in between the stencil side and the pocket side. Slip it into the tail-end for the elephant and either side for the robot. Pin in place.

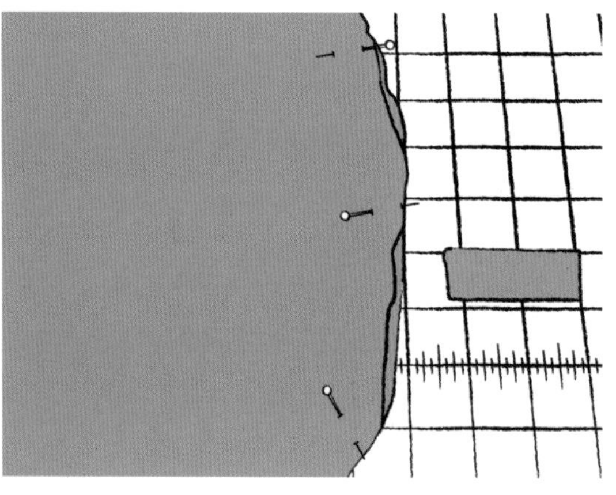
STEP 3

4 Set the sewing machine to a very minimal zigzag stitch (1mm) and sew around the outside with a ½" seam allowance. Leave a 4" opening at the bottom of the pillow. Because the elephant is rounded, clip around the curve. Make sure to not cut too close to the seam.

STEP 4

5 Turn the pillow right side out but with the pocket wrong side out over the stencil. Fill with stuffing.

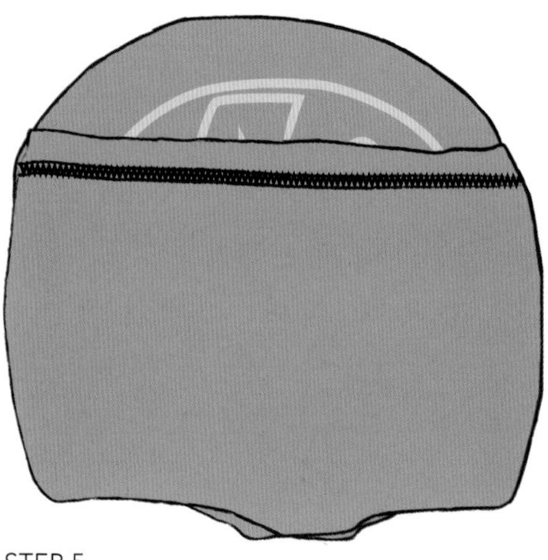
STEP 5

6 Sew along all three layers of the bottom opening. Flip the pocket to the back. Adjust stuffing into corners and you're done!

BLOSSOM BAND

BLOSSOM BAND

Finished dimensions: Adjustable fit

This versatile accessory has the ability to morph from a headband into a wrist cuff in the blink of an eye. Wear it around your neck or slip it on a gift package for instant party spirit. It utilizes clever cast-offs from t-shirts and features favorite bits from your scrap bin.

Make the Band

1 Remove the bottom hem of a t-shirt. Carefully cut above the parallel seams to leave the channel created by the fold. Cut a 28" piece of this channel.

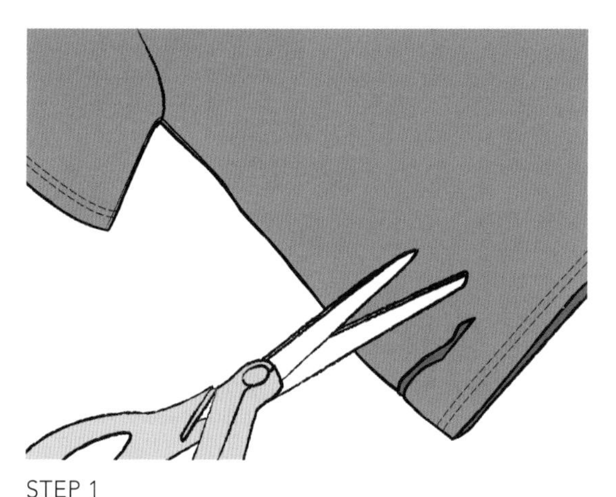

STEP 1

2 Measure the elastic around the wearer's head to assess the amount needed for a snug but comfortable fit. Each kind of elastic has different give, so it's important for you to determine this. Attach a small safety pin to one side and thread it through the channel you cut from the t-shirt. Overlap the two ends of elastic and stitch them together by hand or machine. Adjust the gathers of the jersey and tuck one open end into the other. Stitch together with a simple seam.

SUPPLIES

- Variety of t-shirts
- Thin elastic (less than ½" wide)
- Safety pin
- Fabric selvedge and scraps
- Ribbons, lace, and pieces of favorite odds and ends

Make the Pom-poms

1 Cut two ½" strips of jersey parallel to the hem line.

2 Pull and stretch each one to create a long string with edges that roll inward. Set aside.

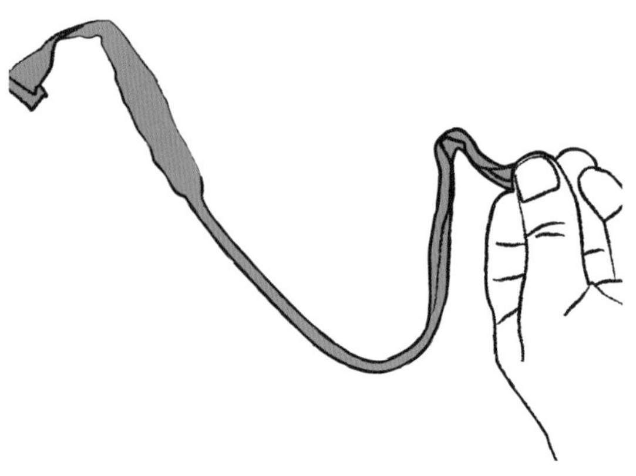

STEP 2

3 Cut out two 2" cardboard circles. Cut a 1" circle out of the center of each to create two rings. (Refer to Chapter 1 for information about making a circle template.)

4 Place the two rings together. Wrap the jersey string around the outer ring. When another piece of string is needed, begin with the edge facing away from the inner circle and continue wrapping until the rings are evenly filled.

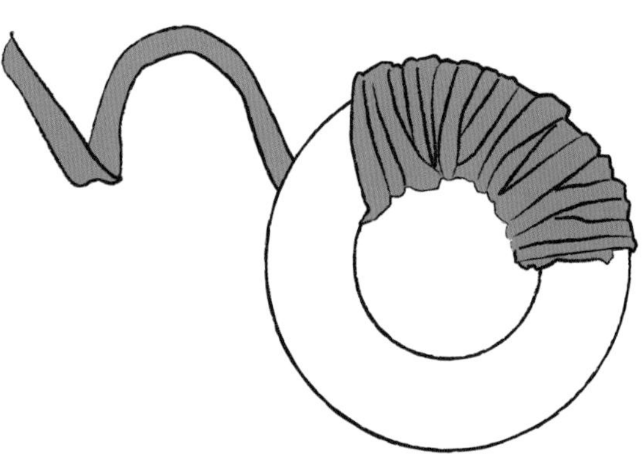

STEP 4

5 Snip the strings where the two rings meet with a pair of scissors. Hold it together securely as you clip.

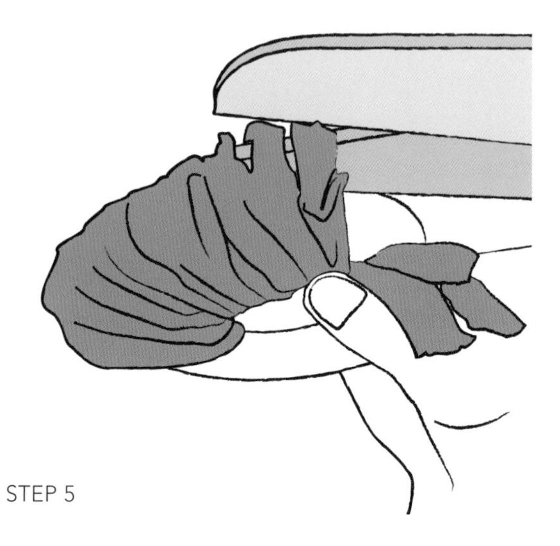

STEP 5

6 Slide a piece of string in between the rings without letting go of the newly snipped loose strands. Use this piece to tie all the snipped pieces together. Now it's looking familiar! Fluff out your pom-pom and trim all the pieces to create a uniform little ball.

7 Make several pom-poms in desired color combination.

Make the Blossoms

1 Make another t-shirt string from a ½" strip cut parallel to the hemline and pulled taut.

2 Fold one loop after another, securing with a needle and thread at the base of each loop.

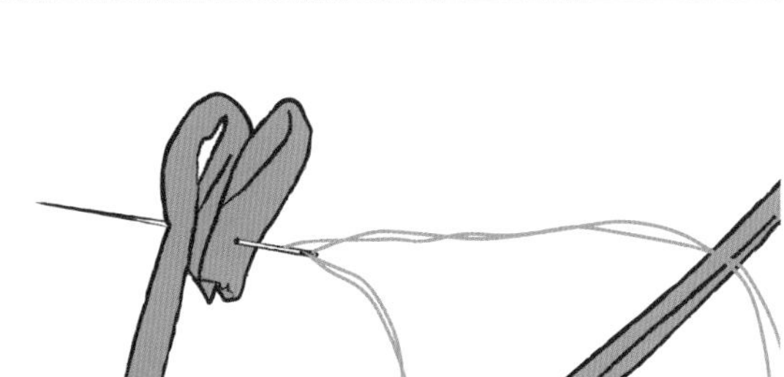

STEP 2

3 Sew 9 to 10 loops and then connect the first loop to the last to form a flower.

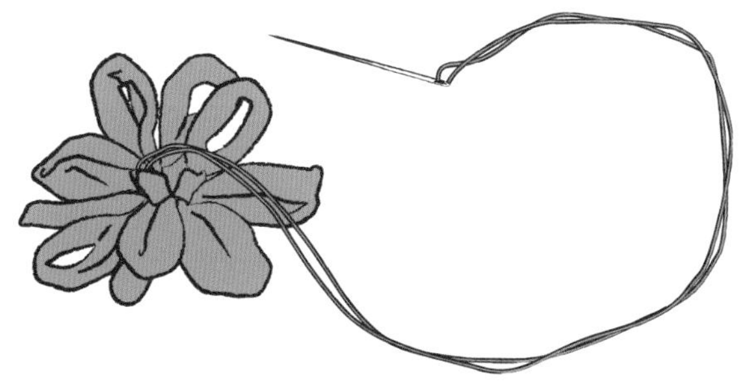

STEP 3

4 Sew the center of the flower directly over the seam on the band where the elastic meets. Add a button to the center for stability and decoration.

Put It All Together

Make each band as simple or abundant as you desire. Stitch and tie ribbon, scraps, flowers, and pom-poms directly to the band.

LITTLE FORAGER SKIRT

LITTLE FORAGER SKIRT

Finished Dimensions: Fits 2–4T and 5–7

Take a child to the shore or down a wooded path, and she'll often gather small shells, stones, and an acorn or two. This soft and comfortable skirt has a built in apron pocket for collecting nature's treasures and is designed for an active explorer. Sturdy ribbons on each side of the skirt slip through apron loops for a secure fit or easy removal when those pockets are full or when unencumbered play calls. Consider stamping the apron and the ribbons with a flower pod to echo the natural bits the wearer carries within her pockets.

NOTE: Although the skirt pictured only uses two colors, this pattern is ripe for collaging multiple shades together. There is wonderful potential for using many different t-shirt scraps if you're in the mood for lots of different color blocks.

SUPPLIES

- 2 or 3 heavy weight 100% cotton men's t-shirts in size XL or XXL in contrasting colors (at least one for the apron and skirt and one for the bias trim)
- 1½ yards 1" twill tape or any favorite sturdy ribbon
- Seam ripper
- ½" elastic cut to fit the skirt's wearer
- Stretch needle
- Fabric stamp pad
- Natural object for printing
- Tailor's chalk
- Rotary cutter and mat
- Scissors
- Pins
- Paper
- Pen
- Soup can or glass with 3" diameter

Make the Apron Pocket

1 Create an apron template using the illustration as your guide. Fold an 8" × 10" piece of paper in half lengthwise with the fold on the left side. Mark 1" from the right side along the top. Mark 2" from the bottom on the open right side. Connect the dots with a ruler and cut along the line.

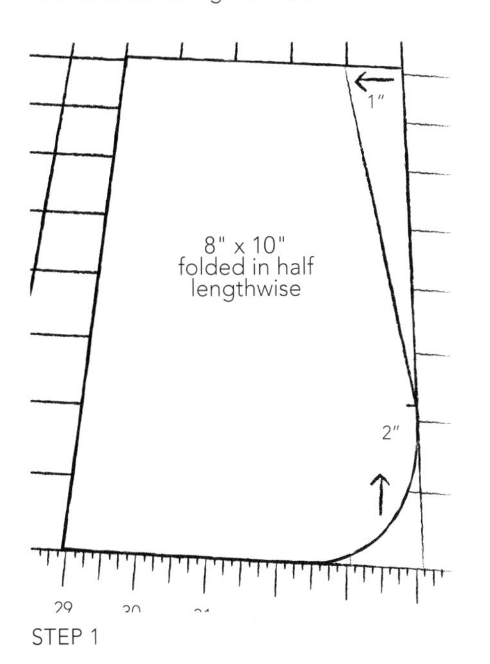

STEP 1

2 Use a soup can in the bottom right corner to round the ends.

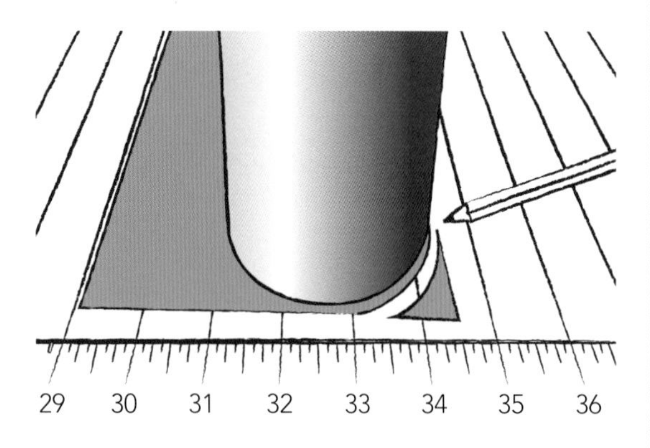

STEP 2

3 Lay the t-shirt you have chosen for the apron and skirt on a flat cutting surface. Smooth out any creases. Just below the neckline, pin the template to the fabric. Cut through both sides of the shirt so that there are two identical pieces. A rotary cutter and mat are helpful.

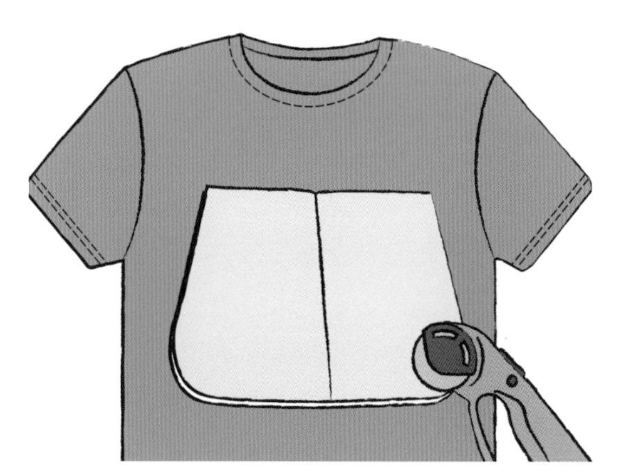

STEP 3

4 Using a ruler and pen, draw a line 2 ½" from the top of one of the pieces. Use scissors or a straight edge and rotary cutter to cut along this line. This smaller piece is the pocket.

5 Make 38" of jersey "bias tape" from the t-shirt that you're using for the trim. (Although it is not cut on a bias as traditional bias tape is, the jersey smoothly stretches around curves to achieve the same effect. I'm calling it bias tape for the purposes of this project.) Neatly snip off the hem of the shirt and then cut 1 ¾" strips of jersey parallel to the hem line. Add length to the strips by sewing the short ends together right side to right side and pressing the seams open.

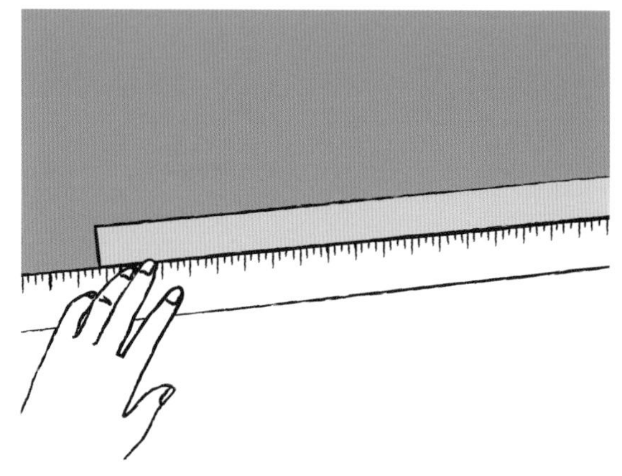

STEP 5

6 Position the bias tape so that one edge is flush with the top edge of the pocket with the right sides facing. Set your sewing machine to a zigzag stitch (3mm) and sew on the bias tape with a ⅜" seam allowance. Fold the tape up and over the top edge of the pocket. Press in place. Topstitch directly onto the bias tape next to the seam you just created. Make sure to catch the back piece with the seam. Trim off the bias tape edges on the same angle as the pocket.

7 Place the pocket on top of the apron piece; both pieces should face right side up. Attach the bias tape to the sides and bottom of both pieces as described in Step 6.

8 Using a straight stitch sew a seam directly down the center of the pocket to divide it in two. Reinforce the top by sewing back and forth several times. Also reinforce the bottom right before the bias tape begins.

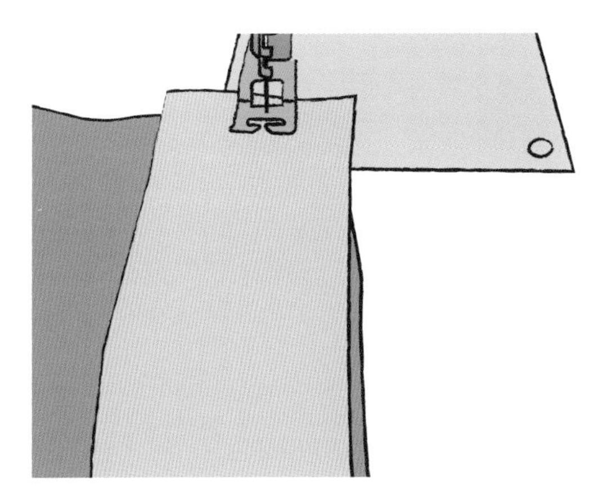

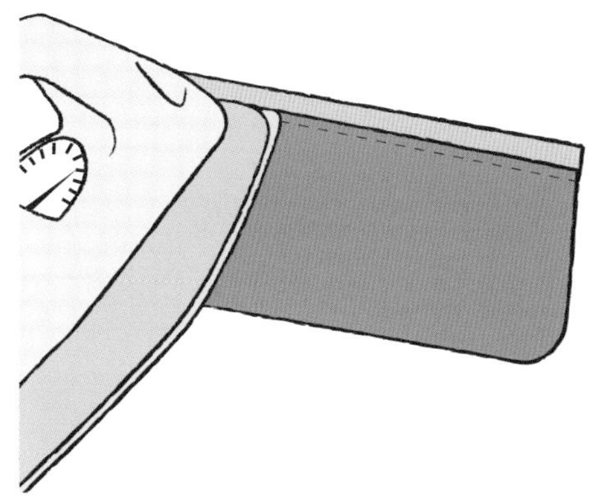

STEP 6

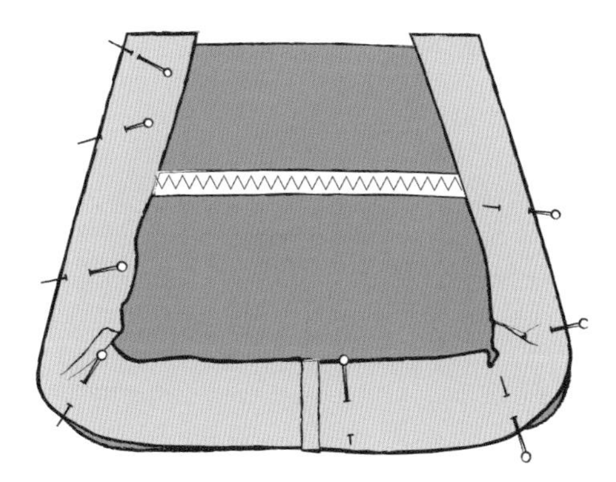

STEP 7

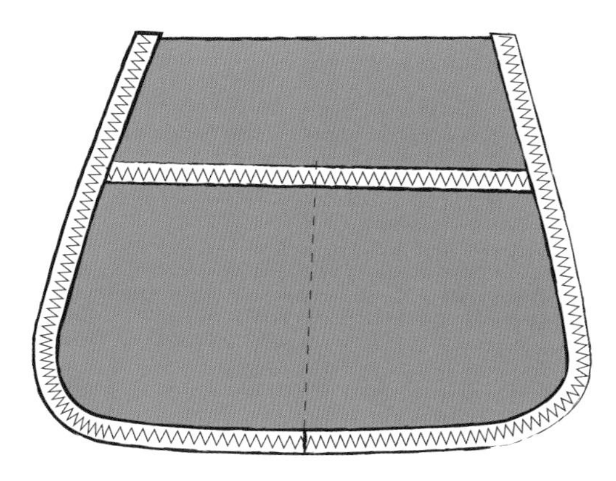

STEP 8

9 Create belt loops with twill tape. Cut four strips of twill tape that are the same length as they are wide plus an extra inch. Place two in a vertical direction adjacent to the sewn-on bias tape on either side. Place the other two evenly spaced closer to the center. For instance, the sample skirt uses 1" twill tape so the four strips are all 2" long.

10 Pin a 10" strip of bias tape along the top of the apron and over each piece of twill tape with a little bias left over on each side. Sew in place as you did with the other bias tape, but when it comes to pressing and folding over, also tuck in the edges so that the raw edges aren't exposed on the sides.

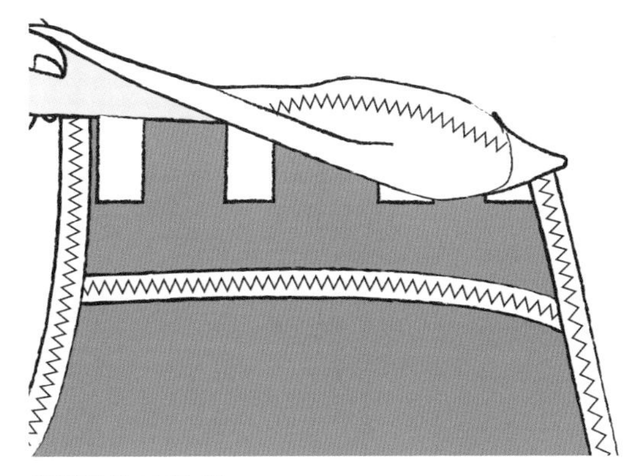

STEPS 9 AND 10

11 Fold under the bottom of each strip of twill tape and sew down to the apron with a straight stitch locked at beginning and end.

12 Embellish apron with printing of your choice. I stamped the sample with poppy pods.

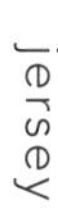

Make the Skirt

1 Cut the sleeves from the shirt the apron was cut out of. If making the larger size (5–7) you might need to use an additional t-shirt.

2 Turn the shirt inside out and lay flat on a cutting surface. Smooth out any creases. Fold the shirt in half so that the side seams touch. If it's a seamless shirt, just estimate where the side seams would be beneath the cut-away sleeve.

3 Mark the cut lines on the t- shirt according to the diagram for the size you are making. Cut out the pieces, making sure to cut through all layers of the t-shirt. Set aside.

4 Prepare strips for the bottom ruffle. Cut two strips according to the diagram's measurements from the bottom of the shirt, parallel to the hemline. Improvisation is encouraged to create the amount of gathering you desire, but the measurements provided will make a soft gathered ruffle as shown on the skirt in the photo.

Size 2-4T

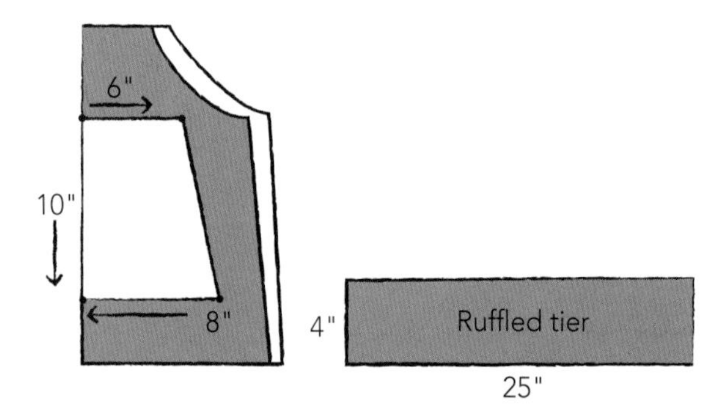

Size 5-7

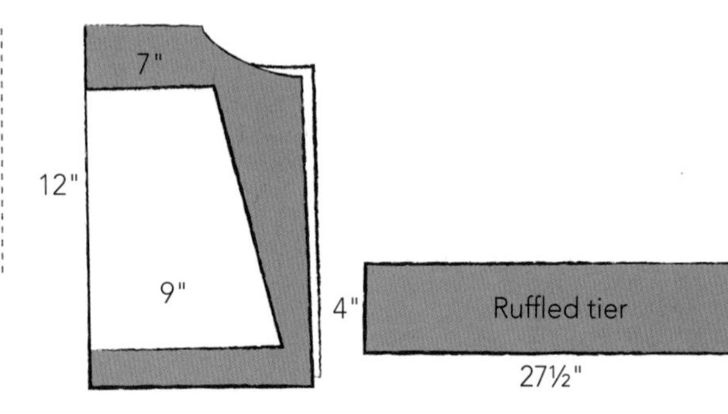

5 Begin constructing the skirt. Keep the cut pieces of the t-shirt with right sides facing. Pin the sides cut on a diagonal. Sew the side seams using a small zigzag stitch and a ⅜" seam allowance.

6 Wrap a length of elastic around the child's waist until it is snug but comfortable. Cut the elastic ½" longer than her waist and overlap the two ends. Stitch together and sew back and forth several times for added strength.

7 Pin where the elastic has been joined to the wrong side of the center of the skirt's back panel. The top of the elastic edge should be flush with the top edge of the fabric. Pin the opposite side of the elastic to the center of the front panel, again pinning on the wrong side of the fabric and with the elastic and skirt edges flush. Pin the elastic to each side seam so that the elastic is evenly distributed in all four pinning locations. You will need to stretch it out to meet both side seams. The elastic should be divided fairly evenly between all four pins.

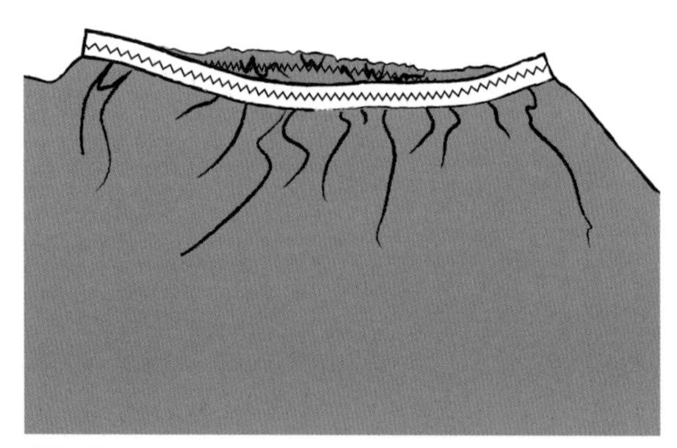

STEPS 6 AND 7

8 Sew directly on the elastic, again using a 3mm zigzag stitch. Pull the elastic as you sew to stretch it along the jersey skirt. Sew around the entire waist and lock your stitches at the end.

9 Fold over the elastic and jersey toward the wrong side. Sew another zigzag stitch along the edge of the bottom of the elastic. Stretch the waistband the entire time you're stitching.

10 Cut two strips of twill tape or ribbon for the side ties. They should each be long enough to reach from the side seam at the waist to comfortably tie at the belly button.

11 Using a seam ripper, carefully open the side seam directly under the elastic waistband; the opening should be just wide enough to slip in each ribbon. The skirt is still turned inside out, so insert the ribbon from the right side about an inch into the opening on the wrong side. Any ribbon design should be facing the back panel, as it will end up being highlighted in front this way. Stitch over the ribbon along the side seam several times for strength.

12 Place the ruffle strips right side to right side and sew up each short side with a small zigzag stitch using a ⅜" seam allowance.

13 Set your machine to the longest basting stitch and sew along the entire top edge to create a gather. (Refer to the gathering instructions in Chapter 1 if you need help.) Gently pull on the thread to gather the ruffle until the top gathered edge is equal in length to the bottom of the skirt. Adjust the gathers for evenness and attach the ruffle to the bottom edge of the main skirt body. Make sure to have the right sides facing and the side seams of the ruffle and skirt matching. Pin the ruffle in place and sew in place just below the gathered seam.

14 Cut more t-shirt bias tape to match the width of the bottom of the skirt and attach it to the bottom hem just as you did for the apron.

15 Pull up her skirt, tie on the apron, and head out for a nature walk!

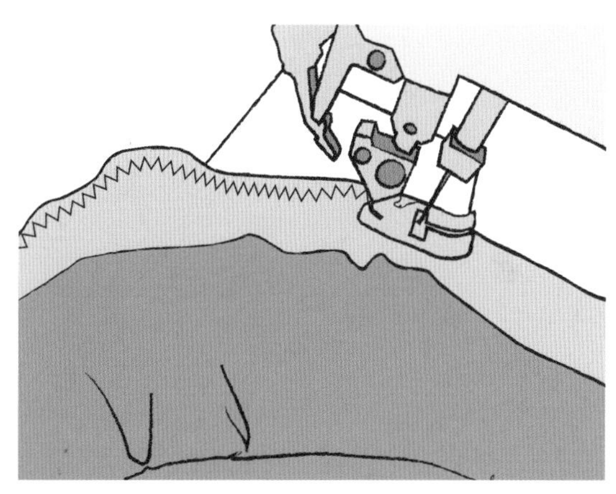

STEP 14

Stone Water Painting

Water painting is a soothing and meditative art practice that can be appreciated at any age but is especially appealing to a young child. Use a flat stone for a canvas, a small paint brush as a tool, and a jar of water for "paint." On a warm day, the heat of the stone dries the water to create a blank surface for each new creation. Collecting stone canvases and filling a jar with water are part of the activity if you choose to paint at the water's edge; however, stone painting can be enjoyed anywhere . . . even in front of a blazing hearth as a reminder of summer days by the shore. ■

BARN THROW

BARN THROW

Finished dimensions: 50" × 70"

No one would ever guess that this simple but elegant throw was made from white promotional t-shirts found in abundance at every thrift shop. Quilted channels of soft jersey make this blanket a cozy addition to your morning cup of tea and just the right weight for summer's in-between weather.

SUPPLIES

6 t-shirts with minimal or no graphics
1 bed sheet
52" × 72" batting
Rotary cutter and cutting mat or scissors
Water soluble marker or 1"-wide painter's tape
2"-wide yardstick
Fabric paint
Stencil
Freezer paper
Craft knife

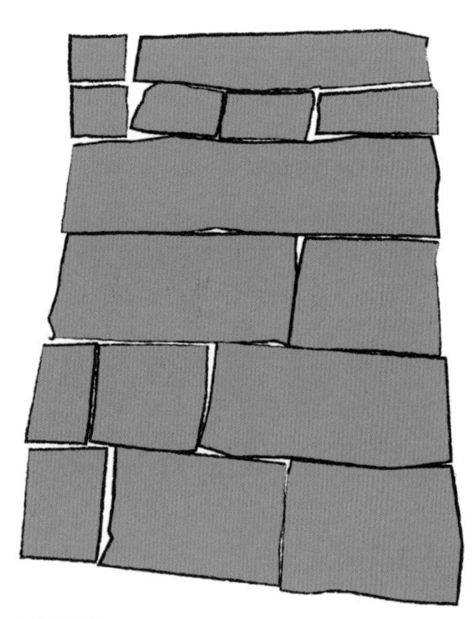

STEP 2

Patchwork

NOTE: In this untraditional quilt, all pieces are assembled with the grain line in the same direction. The most stretch in a t-shirt is from side to side. Long strips of jersey are connected with this side-to-side stretch as the width of the throw. All seam allowances are ¼" unless otherwise stated.

1 Deconstruct t-shirts to get the largest and longest pieces possible. To do this, cut off the sleeves, neckline, and hemline. Discard any graphics to the scrap bin. If it is a seamless shirt, cut up one side to open it, but keep the other intact for a long piece. Cut straight rectangles with a yardstick and rotary cutter.

2 Lay all rectangles on a large floor. Group like widths together. Lay out rows that come close to 52" wide. Create as many rows as needed to come close to 72" long.

3 Sew together the pieces in each row. Trim and adjust the measurements until all rows are the same width and a single row measures 52". Sew each row in this manner. Press open all seams.

4 Lay out all rows again. Make any adjustments necessary, and then begin sewing them together along the 52" sides. Press all seams out again.

Quilt

1 Spread out the batting on the floor. Lay the finished patchwork directly on top of it with the right side up. Smooth out any creases, which takes time and care when you work with jersey. Pin around every side and corner, and also pin in random places in the middle. Don't scrimp on the pins. This is one time to be abundant with pinning so that everything stays stable.

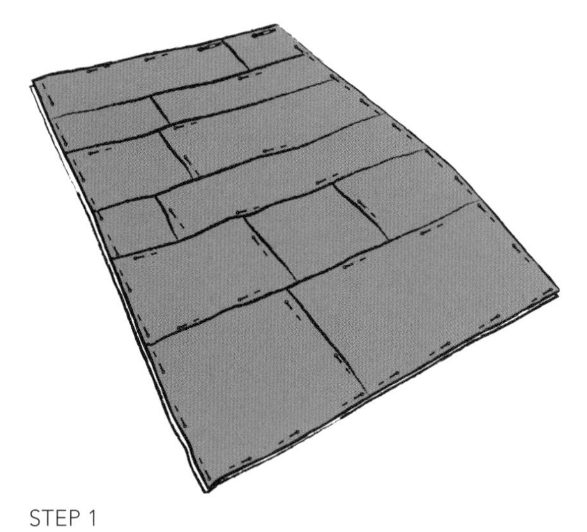

STEP 1

2 Mark quilt lines down the width of the quilt every 1". My two suggested ways to make your marks both rely heavily on a yardstick. If you haven't been to your local hardware store to pick one up, now would be a good time to do so.

- First suggestion: Use a water soluble marker to make long straight lines every 1" directly on the jersey side. Make sure to measure between the top and bottom of the lines to ensure that the 1" remains consistent. When you're finished, stitch down each line with a long stitch (4mm).
- Second suggestion: Use 1"-wide masking or painter's tape. Use the edge of the yardstick to lay it out straight. After securing a piece of tape to the quilt, place the yardstick on top of the tape and lay down the next strip using the edge of the yardstick. There will be a blank 1" between each 1" strip of tape. Sew down the side of each strip of tape with a 4mm-length stitch.

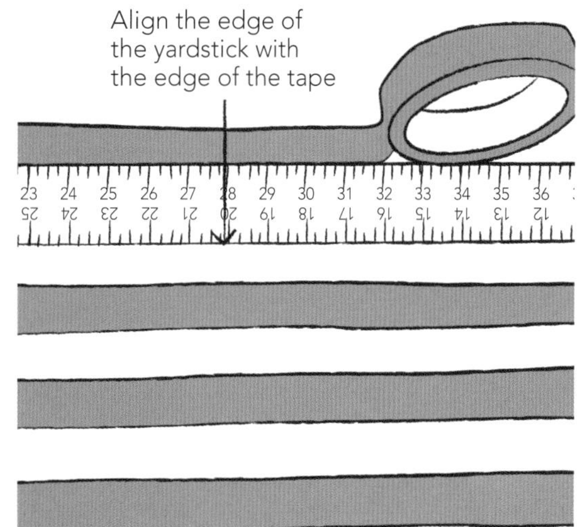

STEP 2

NOTE: Keep these things in mind as you quilt with jersey:

- Jersey has a tendency to stretch when pulled, so gently guide it through your machine.
- Expect a little wonkiness; perfection is not in order with t-shirt quilting. If stitch lines are not completely straight, a little extra character is added to the throw.

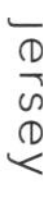

Put It All Together

1 Cut the bed sheet to 51" × 71". Lay the sheet on top of the quilt with the right sides facing. Pin together. Trim off all extra bits of the quilt to match the sheet's dimensions.

2 Sew with a ½" seam allowance around the entire perimeter, leaving an 8" opening for turning.

3 Clip the corners and turn right side out through the opening. Press and pin closed the opening. Press the entire blanket. Stitch all the way around the outside of the quilt ¼" from the edge, closing the opening as you sew. Toss in the washing machine and dryer to set the quilting and finish it.

4 Optional: Add the barn swallow stencil to the sheet side in the position and quantity of your choice. Try a single one in the corner or three soaring together. Heat set.

My Mother's Barn

By the time I went away to college, I had lived in at least 15 different homes. We were rental nomads who dreamed of putting down roots. As a single parent, it took my mother a little longer than some, but a few years ago she finally purchased her very first home. She had always been drawn to non-traditional living spaces, and this new house was just that—a 120-year-old abandoned barn, perched on cement blocks, ripe for rescue and just the right price. As an artist and collector, the barn became her largest canvas.

Always respectful of the building's original form, my mother combined salvaged materials with green building supplies to create a home that reflected her aesthetic as well as her values. The fact that it was down the road from my own little house gave me an opportunity to be very involved in its transformation. So much energy was focused on reshaping and reinventing the building that I hadn't anticipated what it would feel like to settle into the barn as a my mother's home . . . or as my children call it, "Grandma's barn." As she began to open boxes, I realized the magnitude of the unpacking of one's life. She had accumulated treasures from flea markets, yard sales, and markets all over the world. These, along with our humble family heirlooms, had been in storage for decades.

I had always envied friends that were able to return to their childhood homes as adults. Now, I feel as if I have that home to return to. When it came time to photograph the projects for this book, it seemed only natural to use my mom's barn as a backdrop. The barn was her dream come true, and this book is mine.

CHAPTER 6

WOOL

As the oldest natural animal fiber, there has never been a textile that possesses so many favorable qualities as wool. Its ability to insulate and wick away moisture makes it an ideal material for most climates. Wool keeps you warm in the winter, and it's a natural temperature regulator for comfort all year long. It repels dirt, neutralizes odors, and is extremely absorbent. Wool's natural resistance to fire makes it the safest of all household textiles. Because there are so many inherent wonderful qualities in this fiber, I return to it again and again for design inspiration.

History

The early hunter-gatherers were probably the first to discover the beneficial and diverse properties of wool when they wrapped themselves in the skins of wild sheep. In 10,000 BC the first sheep were domesticated in West Asia. It took thousands of years of breeding before sheep's wool was long and soft enough to produce a fiber that could be spun. These wooly sheep weren't introduced to Europe until the Bronze Age. For centuries the production of wool and its industry has flourished all over the world. In the mid 20th century new synthetic textiles, which were celebrated for their ease of care, spurred innovative developments in wool technology. Chemicals were introduced to wool manufacturing to create a competitive wash-and-wear wool—for better or worse.

Sourcing

Blankets and thrifted suits are my rescued wool of choice for the projects in this book. They are soft yet sturdy, and they resist stretching out of shape as sweaters tend to do. Sweaters are knit, rather than woven, which increases their elasticity. If you'd like to try substituting felted sweaters, choose ones that are thick and densely felted. You can find used wool blankets on eBay or Etsy and at army surplus stores. Suiting is available in both the men's and women's sections of thrift stores and comes in a variety of colors. Check labels to ensure that they are 100% wool. Large wool coats felt up to a lovely thickness somewhere between a blanket and typical suit. Wool tweeds offer lots of texture variety and are fun to mix and match.

Deconstructing

- Some vintage wool blankets have satin binding on two or four sides. Remove these before you begin cutting. Blanket-stitched edges (decorative stitching) can be incorporated into projects. I especially enjoy using them in handles and straps.
- Dissect wool jackets, coats, and pants at the seams with a seam ripper. Save hardware and pockets for future reuse. Often satin or silk linings are in place. Remove these as well. To maximize fabric that has shaping darts, carefully remove the stitches from the wrong side of the dart. Iron with lots of steam. Wool has the ability to regain its original pre-darted shape like no other fabric.

Tips

- The thickness of wool blankets makes them ideal for projects where padding, insulation, or protection is required.
- The finer weave of suiting is reminiscent of sheets of crafting felt: smooth, tightly woven, and easy to cut.
- Although both blankets and suiting appear to be semi-felted, they each benefit from a run through a washer and dryer cycle to fully felt them. This ensures that they don't unravel or fray at edges left raw.

Environmental Impact

Wool is a renewable resource, easy to clean, biodegradable, and reusable. When organic or holistic farming practices are in place, it's a wonderful natural fiber to celebrate. However, much of today's wool industry uses harsh insecticides to keep sheep parasite free. Heavy chemicals are used in the processing of wool, which we know severely affects the health of workers and ends up in the water supply. In addition, another damaging outcome of the international wool supply is caused by the sheer number of livestock: more water pollution, degradation of land, and a steep increase of greenhouse gases from methane emissions. Considering the source of your textile is just as important with wool as it is for cotton and denim. Seek out small, local sheep farms and organic wool manufacturers.

WOOL TRIVET

WOOL TRIVET

Finished Dimensions: trivet—8" diameter; coasters—4" diameter

Many sewers shy away from circular sewing in favor of simpler straight stitching. This round trivet enables you to practice circular stitching with the added benefit of producing a beautiful woolen pad that welcomes your hot dishes with its subtle bull's-eye pattern. Quilted concentric circles add a striking element to any design. Try making smaller versions of this trivet to use as coasters, or make a large one to use as a seat pad. This is a very simple project that will beckon you to make multiples to give as gifts.

NOTE: Make sure to wash and dry all wool blankets and suiting before working with them to ensure extra felting. (See the tips section in this chapter's introduction.)

SUPPLIES

- 2 or 3 contrasting colors of thick wool (blanket and/or suiting)
- Contrasting thread
- Pins
- Circle template
- Tailor's chalk

Make the Trivet

1 Create a template on card stock. Make an 8" diameter circle with a 2½" circle directly in the center. Use it to cut out three 8" circles.

NOTE: Refer to Chapter 1 for information on how to make a circular template.

2 Layer all three circles directly on top of one another. If you're not using all the same color wool, think about how you want to arrange the layers. The center layer is visible, and a contrasting color shows up nicely. Pin the three layers together around the perimeter of the stack.

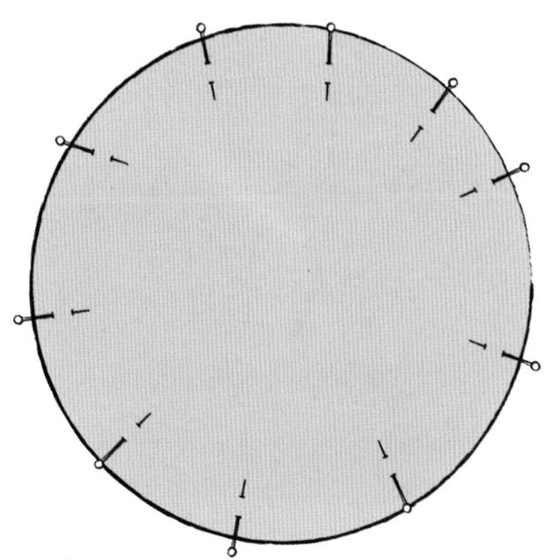

STEP 2

3 Place the template with the hole cut out of the center on the top of your stack of circles. Draw the small center circle with tailor's chalk.

4 Stitch directly on the line of the center circle. Backstitch when the circle is complete.

5 Place the edge of your presser foot on the edge of the center circle and go around again.

6 Keep repeating Step 5 until the circles are ½" from the outer edge. Trim off any uneven pieces of the layers that occurred during the quilting process. Press.

7 Try this same process for coasters using a 4 ½" circular template.

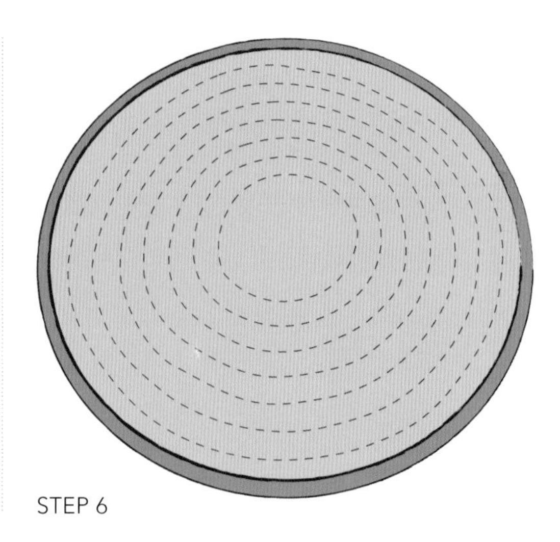

STEP 6

INSULATED LUNCH SACK

INSULATED LUNCH SACK

Finished Dimensions: 12" × 7"

Wool is a wonderful insulator and is naturally water resistant, which makes it ideal for constructing a soft lunch box. Insert an ice pack at the bottom and food will stay cold all day. This sack works beautifully with a stainless-steel tiffin, the traditional lunch box of India that has gained popularity in all parts of the world, but can easily hold a variety of container shapes. If you use a long strap you can sling it over your shoulder to keep your hands free. A short handle works best for children, who might also enjoy the little pocket for holding love notes from their mom or dad.

SUPPLIES

- 1 yard felted wool blanket or thick wool suiting
- Thread
- 5" × 6" piece of tightly woven cotton or linen fabric for the pocket
- 40" of 1½"-wide wool strip for drawstring
- Seam ripper
- Optional: stencil and supplies

Cut the Wool and Batting

1 Using the dimensions shown in the cutting diagram, cut your wool and batting. Read Chapter 1 for simple instructions on creating a circle template.

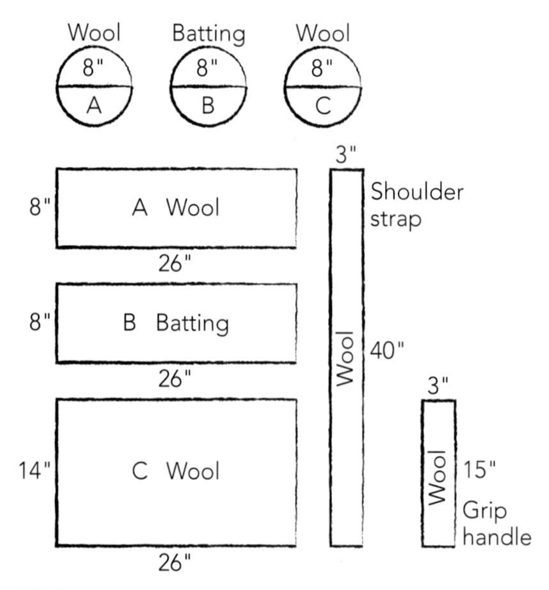

STEP 1

Make the Pocket

1 Fold the top (the 6" side) of your piece of cotton for the pocket ½" to the wrong side and press. Fold another ½", press, and stitch ¼" from the edge of the fold.

2 Fold over each short edge ½" to the wrong side and press. Repeat on the opposite side.

3 Fold the bottom ½" to the wrong side and press.

4 Pin the pocket piece to the center of rectangle A 3½" from the top edge. Begin at the top-right corner and sew all three sides in place ⅛" from the edge of the pocket. Add seams to the right and left sides of the pocket, this time ¼" from the edge.

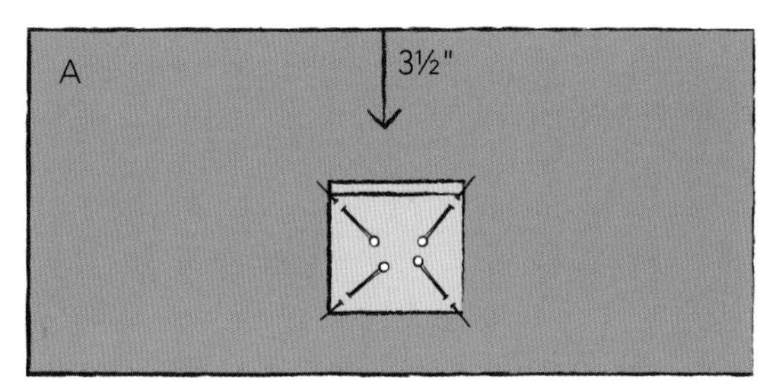

STEP 4

5 Stencil the pocket if desired.

Make the Sack

1 Place batting rectangle A on your work surface and then place wool rectangle B on top of the batting with the pocket facing up. Fold them in half lengthwise with the wool layer on the inside. Sew down the 8" side with a ½" seam allowance.

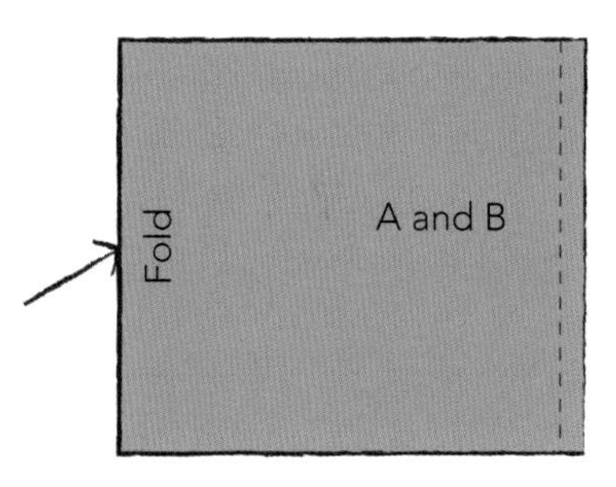

STEP 1

2 Layer circles A and B together and pin them to the tube you created in Step 1 with the batting on the outside. This is the exterior layer of the lunch sack. Sew all around the circumference with a ½" seam allowance. Trim the excess fabric and batting from the edges with pinking shears.

3 Fold rectangle C in half lengthwise and sew the 14" side with a ½" seam allowance. Trim the excess and press the seam flat. Attach circle C in the same manner as you used in Step 2. This will be the interior.

4 Insert the interior into the exterior; the wrong sides will be touching. Fold over the top of the larger bag (the interior that you made from pieces C) 3 ½" and pin it to the exterior piece. Make sure to measure to be certain that it's equally folded all around the sack. C will overlap AB. Use a zigzag stitch to sew directly on the folded-over side along the edge where C meets AB.

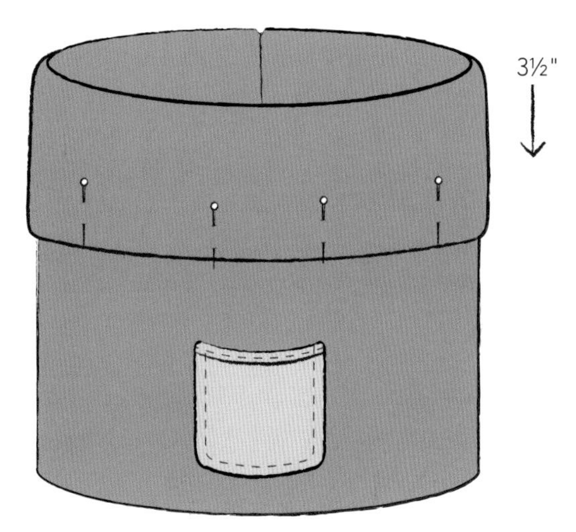

STEP 4

5 Edge stitch around the top opening of the sack. Make a parallel seam 1" from the top. This will be the drawstring channel. Make two vertical ½" slits in the front center of the channel with a seam ripper. Space them 1" apart. Thread the drawstring through the channel.

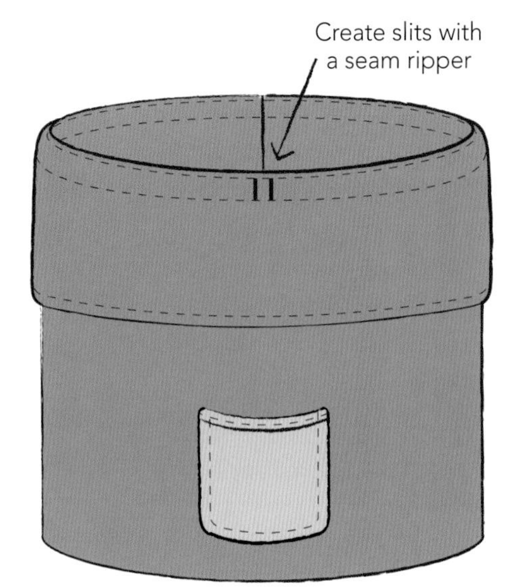

STEP 5

Make a Drawstring

1 Cut a strip of wool that's 36" x 1½" or cut a 36" piece of twill tape. Fold under each 1½" end and stitch in place.

2 Fold the drawstring in half to make a 2" × 1½" rectangle. Zigzag-stitch along the edge to close it.

3 Use a safety pin to run the drawstring through the channel in the lunch sack.

4 Cut a 4" × 1½" piece of wool to make a cinch closure. Fold in half. Sew shut the side opposite to the fold. In the center, zigzag-stitch a seam that runs between the two open sides of the cinch. Edge stitch the folded side. Thread one end of the drawstring through each channel in the closure. Cinch the sack shut.

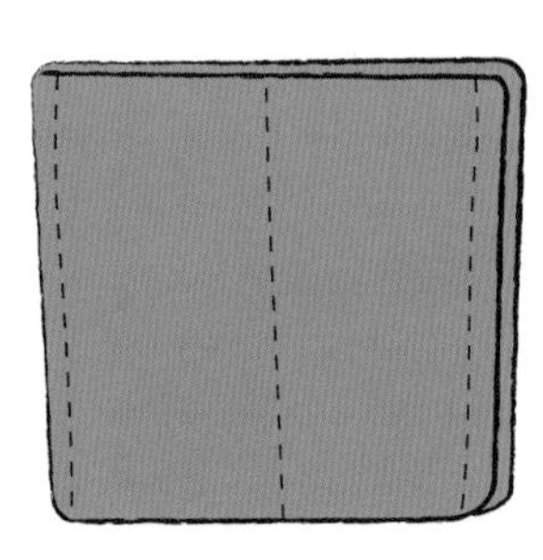

STEP 4

Make and Attach the Handle

NOTE: Cut the wool for the handle or strap to the length desired. In the cutting diagram 40" × 3" is suggested for a long shoulder strap and 15" × 3" for a short handle. I encourage you to discover the measurements that work best for you.

1 Fold the strip in half lengthwise. Zigzag-stitch along the edge of both sides.

2 Find the halfway point on either side of the sack and mark each with a pin 1½" below the seam where the interior and exterior are attached. Fold under one end of the handle 1½"and pin it at the position you marked with the pin. Repeat with the other end of the handle. (Make sure the handle isn't twisted.) Attach the handle to the lunch sack with a boxed X.

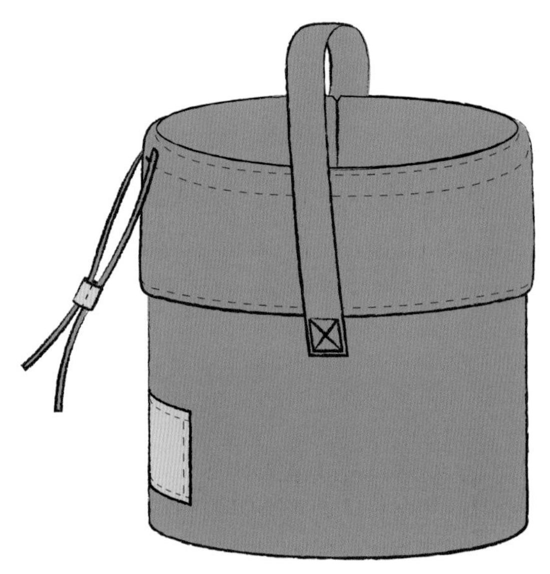

STEP 2

Boy Meets Bag

I rediscovered the amazing insulation properties of wool when I switched to stainless steel lunch containers. I had purchased a two-tiered tiffin (see the "Resources" section for more information) for our 12-year-old son's midday meal. Finding the right cooler to transport it in was proving to be difficult. I wanted to make one but wasn't sure what fabric would be leak proof and insulated without using plastic or vinyl, two materials I was determined to stay away from. My inspiration ended up coming from an unlikely source: the wool soakers my children wore over their diapers when they were babies. From this experience, I knew that wool would keep the moisture in, and I was fairly certain it would insulate well, too. I rummaged through my stash of recycled felted sweaters, but nothing seemed quite "cool" enough for my almost-teenaged boy. Then I remembered a vintage wool army blanket hiding on a top shelf in my studio. It met his approval instantly, and I got to work making a basic design that I hoped would hold up to the rough-and-tumble life of an older boy's lunch sack. This photo shows it one year later . . . after it was used every school day.

Here's what we learned instantly: *Even on really hot days, an ice pack stays colder in two layers of wool than it ever did in any vinyl cooler we'd used in the past.*

Here's what we discovered after months of use by a seventh grader: *Absolutely no leaking, no odors, and amazing durability. Truly, the upkeep is minimal.*

The bonus: *Compliments will abound.* ■

POUFS

POUFS

Finished Dimensions: Small pouf—7½" × 11½" • medium pouf—9½" × 15½" • large pouf—11½" × 23½"

I originally designed the smallest pouf for a play space at a local children's store. I called them Squat Dots because they made perfect spots for sitting and were sized just right for little bodies. They were so well received I thought grown-ups might enjoy them, too. Whether used as a soft stool, a mini ottoman, or a floor cushion, these cozy poufs are versatile and inviting. A variety of sizes encourage lounging, putting up your feet, and stacking. Each one sports a handle for convenient toting from room to room. A simple-to-insert-zipper makes cleaning easy. The best part: the stuffing options! Fill each one with myriad soft items, including all of the scraps from the projects in this book! The largest size makes a wonderful hidden storage unit for extra blankets and guest linens. Wherever they go, these poufs combine style with function.

	Small	Medium	Large
2 wool half circles for bottom*	12" diameter	16" diameter	24" diameter
1 wool circle for top	12"	16"	24"
1 wool rectangle for sides	8" × 37"	10" × 49"	12" × 72"
1 wool rectangle for handle	3" × 8½"	3" × 10½"	3" × 12½"
Zipper	9"	12"	20"

*See Step 2 in the "Prepare the Pieces" section for information on adding an extra ½" to the half circles.

Prepare the Pieces

1 Make a paper circle template using the circle-making instructions in Chapter 1.

2 Fold the paper circle in half and pin it to your wool. Cut along the curve but add an additional ½" before cutting across the diameter (the straight side). (See the illustration on the next page.)

3 Cut out the rest of the pieces of wool and set aside all of them except for the handle.

4 Fold the handle piece in half lengthwise with the wrong sides facing and sew along the side edges. Trim any uneven edges with a rotary cutter and ruler.

SUPPLIES

- Wool (use the size chart to determine how much you need for each pod)
- Zipper (refer to chart for length)
- Ruler
- Roll of paper
- Scissors
- Rotary cutter
- Seam ripper
- Pencil
- Coordinating thread
- Stuffing material

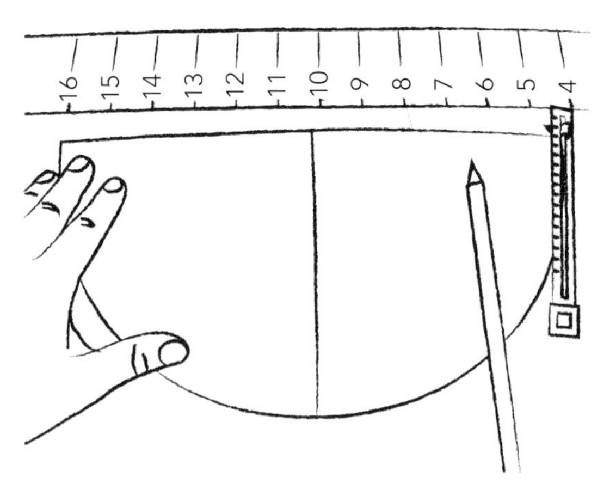

STEP 2

Insert the Zipper

1 Place the two semicircles right side to right side. Baste along the diameter ½" from the edge.

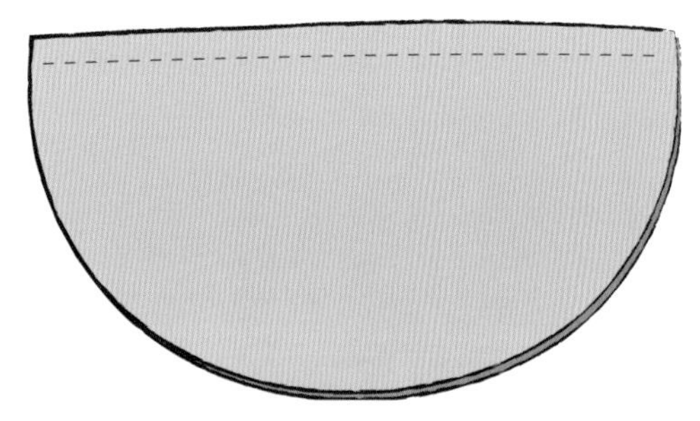

STEP 1

2 Press open the seam with an iron and lay the zipper face down over seam. Mark the two end points of the zipper by inserting pins into the wool at precisely those spots. Set the zipper aside.

3 With right sides facing again, machine stitch the seam at each end (over the basting stitches) starting at the edge and going to the pin markers. Backstitch to secure the seam.

4 Open the seam allowance once more and lay the zipper face down. Make sure that the zipper teeth are exactly over the seam. Pin the zipper in place.

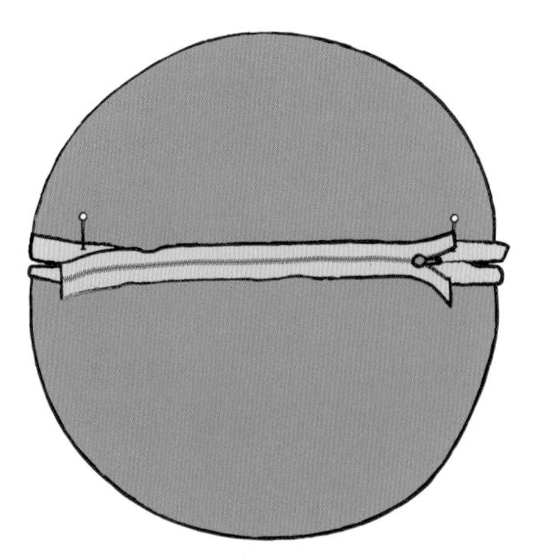

STEP 2

5 Attach a zipper foot to your sewing machine. Starting on the right side stitch ¼" from the seam around the entire zipper. Sew over the bottom and top of the zipper several times.

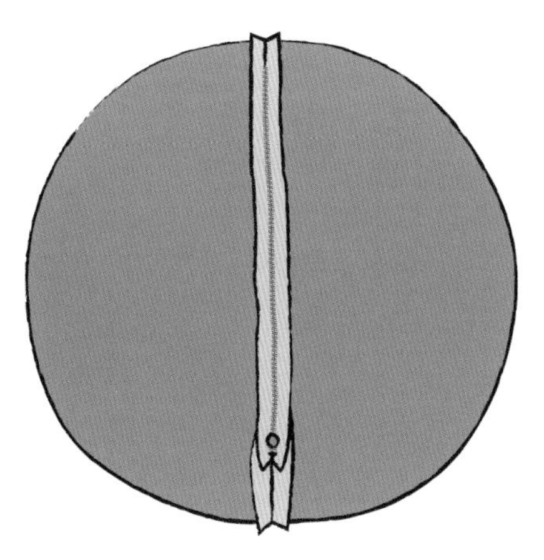

STEP 5

6 Use a seam ripper to remove the basting stitches and make sure that the zipper opens properly. Set this piece aside.

Assemble the Pouf

1 Fold the wool rectangle for the side wall in half with the right sides facing. Sew the short side shut with a ½" seam allowance to form a wide tube.

2 Turn the tube right side out and place the handle directly over the seam. Baste the ends of the handle directly over the center of the seam line. Turn inside out once more.

3 Pin the top circle (the one without the zipper) to one of the openings of the tube. Ease around the curves to ensure that the edges of both pieces line up. Sew in place with a ½" seam allowance. Go around the circle a second time with a parallel seam to ensure durability. Clip the seams around both circles. (See Chapter 1 for information on clipping seams.)

4 Unzip the zipper, line up the tube's seam with the zippered circle's seam, and repeat Step 3. (It's critical that you unzip the zipper for the last step of turning the pouf right side out.) Sew two parallel seams around the circle to complete the pouf.

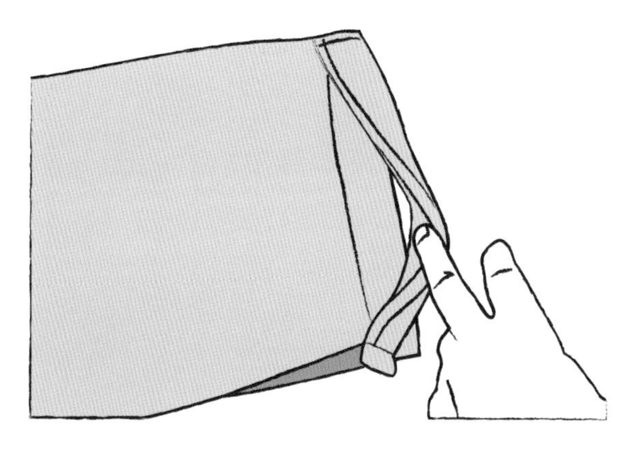

STEP 2

5 Turn the pouf right side out and stuff firmly with filling. Everyday use packs down the contents, which creates a dense cushion. Add more stuffing according to your preferences and enjoy!

TOADSTOOL COTTAGE

TOADSTOOL COTTAGE

Finished dimensions: 9" × 13"

A cardboard tube and scraps of wool are all that's needed to create a cozy home for fairy folks, small dolls, and all the woodland creatures in your playroom. This cottage is sure to enchant all children and even their grown-ups. The roof lifts off for furniture rearranging, and the cottage's circular shape encourages cooperative play among more than one child. There's nothing quite like a handmade toy, and this one is built for years of imaginative play. I know, because I made the first one long ago for my daughter's third birthday and it has been loved by all.

Make the Cardboard Cottage Frame

1 Measure and mark 7" from the bottom of the tube in several spots around the outside. Make a continuous line around the perimeter and cut with a serrated knife. You should now have a 7"-tall tube.

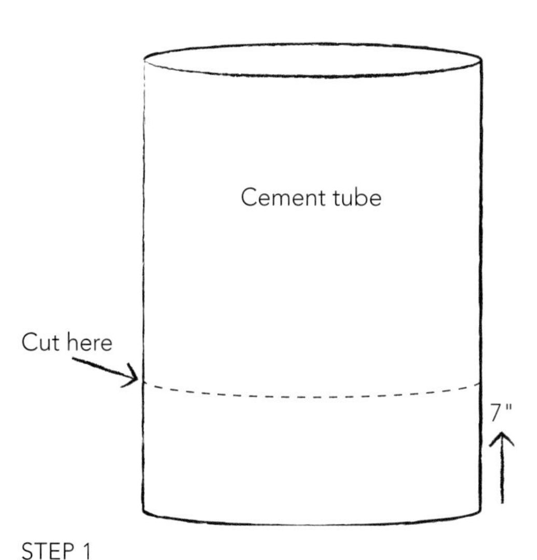

STEP 1

2 Create a paper pattern. Measure the distance around the tube. It will be approximately 32" if you are using a 10" tube. Cut a piece of paper 32" × 7". In the center, along the bottom edge, draw an arched doorway 4" high. Draw two circles for windows in locations of your choice. The sample cottage has a large window in back and a smaller one to the right of the door. Cut out the window circles and door arch and set these shapes aside.

SUPPLIES

- Felted wool blanket or thick wool suiting in red and white (and felt of your color choice for the door)
- Stuffing of choice (I used wool roving)
- Red yarn
- Tapestry needle
- Cardboard (a pizza box works well)
- A section of cardboard tube used for cement forms, which is available at home improvement stores. I recommend 10" diameter, but use what's available and modify the directions accordingly.
- Buttons
- White ribbon
- Serrated knife
- Pen
- Roll of large paper
- Scissors
- Hot glue gun

3 Place the pattern around the tube and tape it in place. Trace the doorway and windows and remove the pattern. Cut out the doorway and windows with the serrated knife. Don't worry if they are a little rough, as you will be covering them with fabric.

Make the Woolen Walls

1 Pin the paper pattern to a section of white wool. Trace the windows and doors and cut them out.

2 Using one of the cut-out paper sections of the door, trace a slightly larger one onto felt of choice. If you're using thin felt, double the thickness to make a sturdier door. If you want, you can cut out a window in the top of the door. Zigzag-stitch around the window. Also zigzag-stitch around the entire door. Attach the door to one side of the white wool door opening with a tight zigzag or button stitch. Add a tiny button for a door knob.

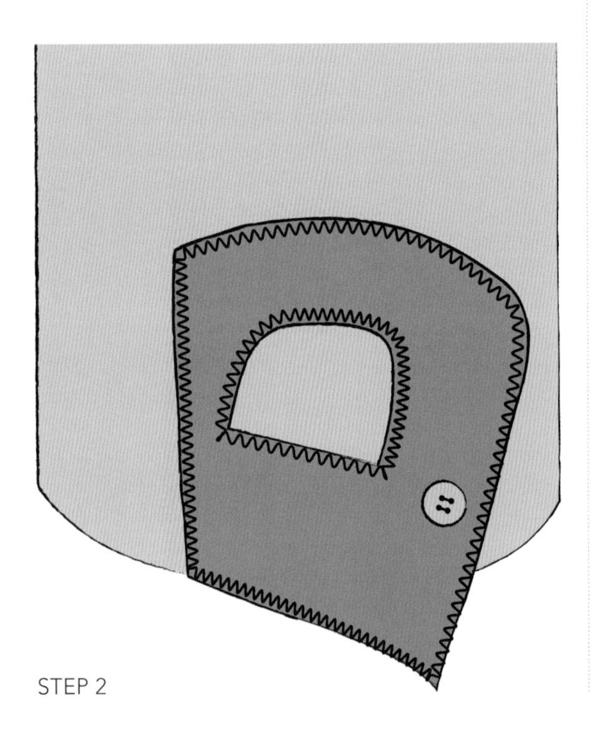

STEP 2

3 Machine stitch or embroider vines beneath the windows. Top them with flower-like buttons to create a garden. Use the same stitch to frame around the window opening,

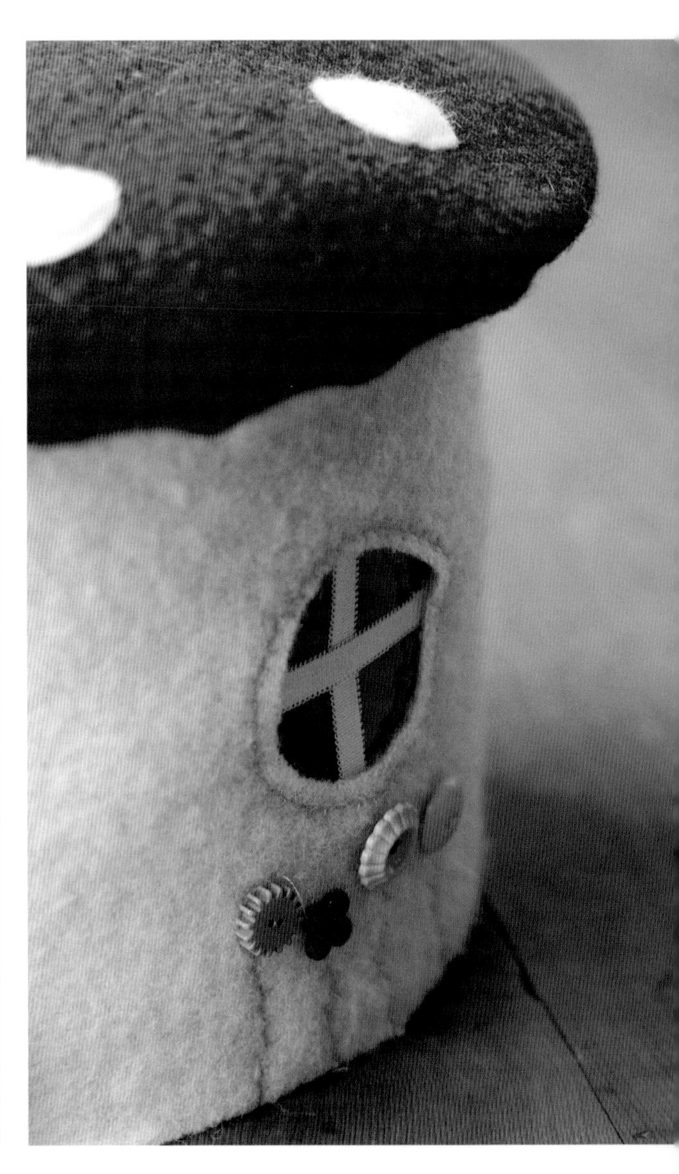

4 Wrap the white wool you cut for the walls around the tube and center it over the doorway and windows. Pull it taut so that one side slightly overlaps the other edge. Pin in place and slip the sleeve of wool off of the tube.

5 Using a tight zigzag stitch sew straight down the overlap to "fuse" both sides together.

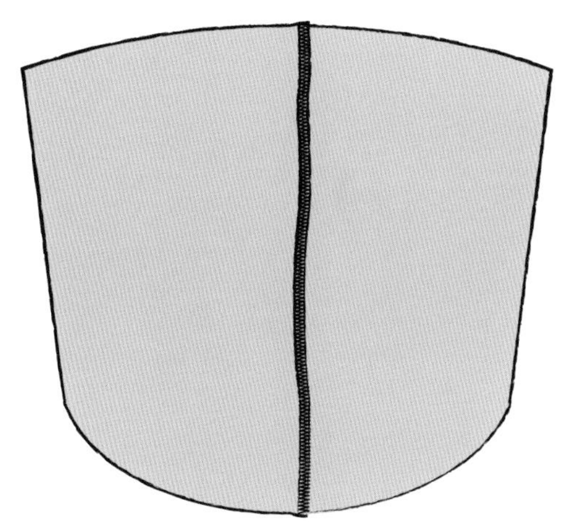

STEP 5

6 On the exterior of the cardboard, hot glue strips of ribbon across the windows to create a crossbar.

7 Slip the woolen wall over the cardboard and adjust so the windows and door are aligned. Use a few dots of hot glue to set the wool in place

Make the Roof

1 Cut a 16"-diameter circle of red wool.

2 Cut nine 1½" circles of white felt. Sew them randomly to the top of the red circle. Use a zigzag stitch and stretch them out slightly in different directions to give them an organic feel.

3 Cut a 13"-diameter circle from a piece of cardboard.

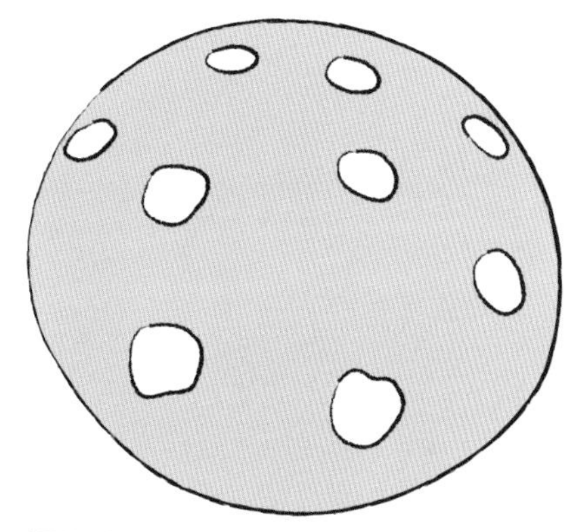

STEP 2

4 Using a tapestry needle and red yarn, hand-sew a running stitch around the perimeter of the red circle. Pull gently to gather and slip over the cardboard circle. Stuff the roof with a little wool or batting to give height and dimension. When you're satisfied with the shape, pull the running stitch taut. Knot it.

5 Optional: Finish the roof with a red woolen circle 12" in diameter. Hand-sew in place so that cardboard is sandwiched in the middle and invisible. Done!

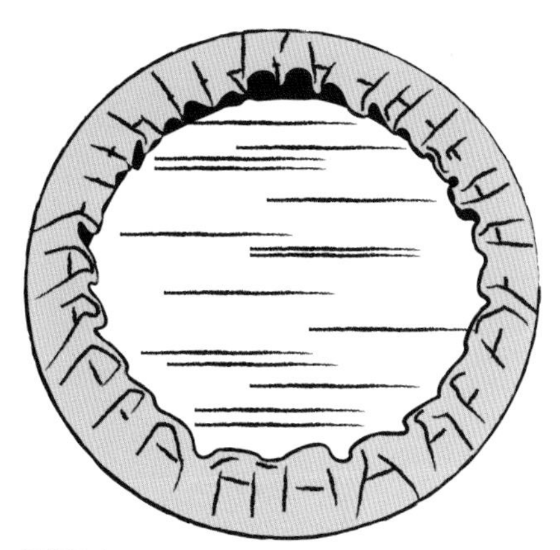

STEP 4

CHAPTER 7

DENIM

Comfortable, strong, and durable—denim has always been the unpretentious fabric of choice for work clothes and blue jeans. When I was growing up in San Francisco, Levi Strauss, the founding father of blue jeans, was a household name. I remember well my first pair of "Levis 501 blues." They were a rite of passage for all eighth graders. We'd head down to the only place in the city that carried our size. It was called The Gap. It was the very first one and would become the next big name in the story of jeans. And that pair of 501's . . . they were also one of my first sewing machine successes—I pegged the legs; a precursor to skinny jeans.

History

Denim first gained popularity during the California Gold Rush when Levi Strauss used it to make "waist overalls" for miners. In the 1930s cowboys and western movies added to the appeal of Levi's jeans. During World War II, American servicemen took their favorite jeans along and spread their popularity overseas. In the 1950s and '60s, TV, film, and the protest movement changed the image of jeans once again to represent youth, rebellion, and individuality. With the advent of "designer jeans" in the 1980s, denim became a high fashion fabric. Today denim has the ability to wear many hats.

Sourcing

Begin the search in your own closet. For small projects, children's outgrown jeans might be just right. In fact, the oven mitt on page 116 was created with my son's old jeans. For larger designs, such as the hammock or tote bag, seek out pants with the most fabric possible. Long, wide-legged ones are very desirable. For reinventing, don't think skinny jeans . . . the bigger the better. The racks of thrift stores and consignment shops are always overflowing with cast-off jeans.

Deconstructing

- Turn any pair of jeans inside out and you'll notice the diagonal weave of contrasting threads; the signature of denim. This reverse side has a softer and more subtle palette that I utilize in many of my repurposed designs. It elevates an otherwise ordinary material and lends a bit of sophistication.
- Working with jeans requires cleverness and the ability to make the most of what you have. Large pieces of usable fabric are possible with patch-working, and smaller projects are determined by the length and width of the legs.
- Jeans are designed to fit the form of your body, therefore the front and back of each leg are sized differently.
- Cut off the bottom hem of each leg. Open up the seam on the outer thigh with a seam ripper. The seam along the inner thigh tends to be topstitched and has to be cut away or incorporated into projects.
- Take measurements at the widest section of the leg to see its sizing potential.
- Although a rotary cutter and ruler cut straight lines, keep in mind that certain parts of the leg are shaped on the bias and this affects your denim strip, potentially adding some unwanted curves.
- Another option is to use the rip technique I enjoy so much. Cut a small snip into the bottom of the leg where the hem was removed. Tear at the snip, and the denim should easily make a clean, straight rip directly up the leg. Continue to make snips equally spaced from one another all along the bottom of the leg. Cut each strip off just below the pocket. This gives you a nice supply of denim strips.

Tips

- A universal sewing needle works with most pairs of jeans, but a specialized denim needle might be helpful with a very thick pair.
- Sew slowly over bulky seams in denim. I turn my wheel by hand if I think a particular seam will be a challenge.

Environmental Impact

Jeans, just like t-shirts, are a wardrobe staple all over the world. If everyone knew the true price of a single pair of jeans, many would think twice before purchasing. The same cotton issues highlighted in the "Jersey" chapter apply to jeans, except you can add 1,500 gallons of water needed to produce only one pair. When we think of denim, we think blue, but jeans are actually white until dyed with heavy metals and toxins that end up flooding the water systems and contaminating the soil adjacent to the manufacturing plants that are predominantly located in third-world countries. It's important to know the origins of our clothing so that our choices are compatible with our beliefs.

DOUBLE DUTY OVEN MITT

DOUBLE DUTY OVEN MITT

Finished dimensions: 6" × 26"

As an avid baker, I'm very particular about my oven mitts. Discovering the inherent insulating properties of wool inspired me to design my ideal mitt. Denim, with its sturdy weave and easy care, is a wonderful workhorse in the kitchen. As I'm always setting a mitt down and forgetting where its partner is, I like the idea of one mitt that does the work of two. It hangs over the oven rail at the ready, needing no extra hand for slipping it on. That's very helpful if you're in a hurry to get those cookies out at the perfect golden time! Each pocket serves as a frame for a monogram, design, or, in this case, common baking temperatures in bold black. The underside gets spotlighted each time something is taken out of the oven. To add interest, I created striping in a carefree layout. Denim and fabric paint are such good friends.

Preparing and Stenciling the Fabric

1 Using the dimensions in the Supplies list, cut all four rectangles from the legs of a pair of jeans and the rectangle of wool (which will serve as a lining in the mitt).

NOTE: For this project, I considered the reverse side of the denim as the right side. The lighter shade creates a wonderful contrast with the black fabric paint.

2 Fold the circle template in half and line up the edge of the circle with the edge of each short side of the rectangles. Use this as a guide for cutting rounded edges.

SUPPLIES

- 2 7" × 27" pieces of denim
- 2 7" × 9" pieces of denim
- 7" × 27" piece from a wool blanket
- 7"-diameter circle template
- Scissors or rotary cutter
- Long straight edge or ruler
- Cutting mat
- Craft knife
- Freezer paper
- Iron
- Textile paint

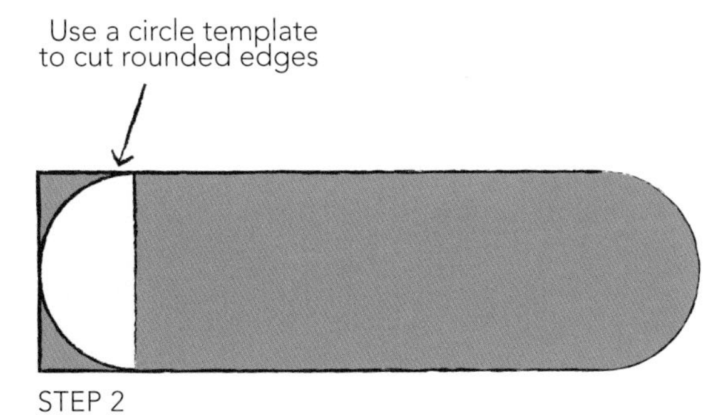

STEP 2

3 Finish the straight 7" side of each 7" × 9" rectangle. To reduce the chance of future unraveling, sew a zigzag stitch or mock overlock right along the edge. Fold over ½" and press. Place the presser foot along the folded edge and use it as your seam allowance. Sew with a straight stitch.

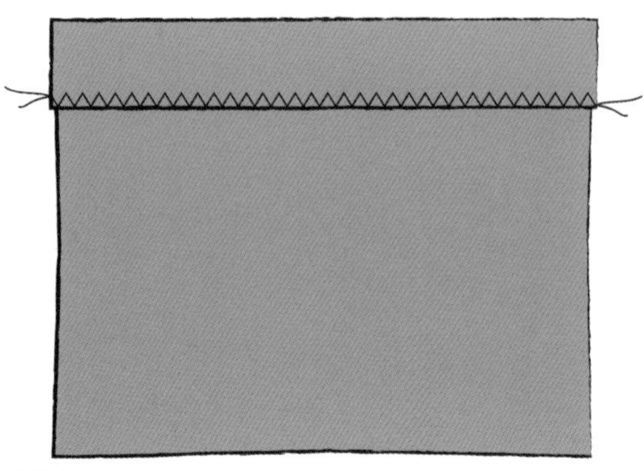

STEP 3

NOTE: A double-fold would keep the fray away, but it creates too much bulk for sewing the wool and denim together later on.

4 Create striping on one of the long rectangles of denim with strips of freezer paper. Cut at least 10 thin 28" (or longer) strips of freezer paper. The widths may vary; ¼" was my average thickness. A long straight edge and cutting mat are very helpful for this part. Arrange the strips on the denim. Keep in mind that the space in between the paper will be filled with paint (the stripes). By varying the width of the paper and the amount of space in between the paper strips, you can achieve a playful, one-of-a-kind striping with less effort than trying to make each strip equally spaced.

5 When you have determined a general idea of the layout, iron on each strip one at a time. Use a ruler to make sure that each stripe remains vertical and doesn't sway too much to one side. Cover the entire piece with paint. Dry and heat set.

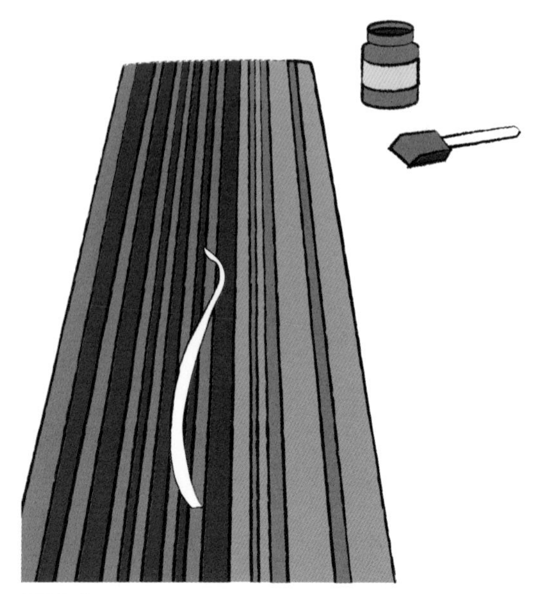

STEP 5

Assemble the Mitt

1 Make a sandwich out of all of the pieces: Lay the striped piece right side up. Next lay the blank piece of denim right side down. The wool comes next. Finally, lay the pockets right side down on top of the wool. Make sure the hemmed sides are straight and even.

2 Pin in place.

3 Sew around the entire perimeter with the presser foot as a seam allowance guide. Leave several inches open for turning in the center of the mitt. Clip all of the rounded edges.

STEP 3

4 Turn the mitt right side out and arrange the pockets on the side opposite of the striping.

5 Pin the opening closed and iron the entire mitt.

6 Sew the opening shut with a blind stitch.

Stencil the Pockets

Stencil numbers or the design of your choice on the pockets. Keep in mind that the folded edge is the top and the rounded side is the bottom for each! Dry and heat set. You're finished and ready for baking!

Cookie Couple

Long before our children came along, and way before marriage, my husband and I went into business together. We had a cookie business—a giant vegan chocolate chip cookie business! We traveled the country, often selling them at Grateful Dead concerts. The day before a show, we would gather our mountain of ingredients and bake 1,000 cookies. 1,000 cookies at one time! It was just the two of us—I mixed by hand; he operated the oven. We had a beautiful system and a lovely rhythm, but by day's end our legs could barely hold us, and we'd collapse smelling like vanilla and brown sugar. Several years later the grand total of baked cookies was near 30,000. We had our favorite baking tools—in fact we still have the spatula—but we never found that just-right oven mitt.

Reinvention Cookies

Although we enjoyed our original vegan cookies, this recipe is loved by everyone in our family and has been my personal favorite for the last few years. It's delicious no matter what the interpretation is. In other words, it works with whatever you might have on hand. We've made it with either butter or oil, with eggs or not, even substituting raisins for chips . . . no matter the combination, these cookies are always delicious!

Preheat oven to 350°

Cream wet ingredients:

- ½ cup of butter or vegetable oil of choice
- 1 cup of cane sugar
- 1 Tablespoon of molasses
- 1 egg or egg substitute
- 1 teaspoon of vanilla

Blend dry ingredients:

- 1 cup of rolled oats (whole or pulverized into oat flour in a food processor—both versions are great!)
- 1 cup of whole wheat pastry flour
- ½ teaspoon baking powder
- ½ teaspoon baking soda
- ½ teaspoon salt

Mix wet and dry ingredients together. Add a cup of chocolate chips or raisins. Drop spoonsful of dough onto a cookie sheet and bake for 10 minutes. Rotate to different oven racks while baking for even browning. Cool and enjoy!

Here are other additions we've loved:

- Chips, dried cranberries, and orange zest
- Coconut and dried pineapple pieces
- Diced crystalized ginger and chocolate chunks ■

INDI-GO BAG

INDI-GO BAG

Finished Dimensions: 21" × 15"

This will be your go-to bag when heading out on your next adventure. Tough and rugged denim, utilized for its strength and easy care, is just what's needed on a trek to the beach or a bike ride to the farmer's market. Transform a pair (or two) of jeans into a simple but refined carry-all. The familiar and common become fresh and unique by using the "wrong side" of the denim as the exterior. The paler weave is highlighted and creates a wonderful foil for contrasting thread.

SUPPLIES

- 1–2 pairs of jeans with matching interior weaves
- Contrasting thread (red or orange work nicely)
- Pillow case or ½ yard of other lightweight cotton that coordinates with the contrasting thread
- Scissors
- Zipper foot (optional)
- Ruler
- Tailor's chalk

NOTE: To create this tote, you need one to two pairs of jeans, depending on their size. The legs provide long continuous strips of material that are sewn together to create a large piece of fabric. Because jeans have been designed to conform to the shape of bodies, they are cut with curves in the legs. This is a straight and boxy tote, so it's important to establish the grain line of the strips. The simplest method is ripwork: Tear the legs into equal vertical strips beginning at the hemline. Ripping is quick and satisfying and the result is the perfectly straight pieces necessary for the structure of this particular bag. Although the exact dimensions are provided, feel free to improvise a new size using the denim that you have on hand.

Preparing the Strips

1 Cut the hem off of the pant legs. Make a vertical snip parallel to the outer leg seam. Rip all the way up to the pocket. Measure 4" over and make another vertical snip. Rip and repeat.

2 Continue until there are enough strips to cut 12 4" × 10" lengths. You need 6 for each side of the bag.

3 Prepare the bag's base by cutting a 12" × 22" section of a jean leg. Set this rectangle aside.

4 Rip two 2" × 22" pieces for the top bands of the bag.

5 Rip two 6" × 30" pieces to make the handles. Press each strip in half lengthwise with the blue jean side in. Open the strips and fold each end to the center crease mark. Fold in half again and press. Edge stitch down the length of both sides. Set the straps aside.

NOTE: In these instructions the inside of the denim is called the right side, and the outside of the jeans is referred to as denim.

Assemble the Exterior of the Bag

1 Take two 4" × 10" strips and place the denim sides together. Pin and sew a ¼" seam down the length of one side. Connect a total of six strips in this manner. Set this six-strip piece aside and repeat the same steps with the other six 4" × 10" strips for the other side of the bag.

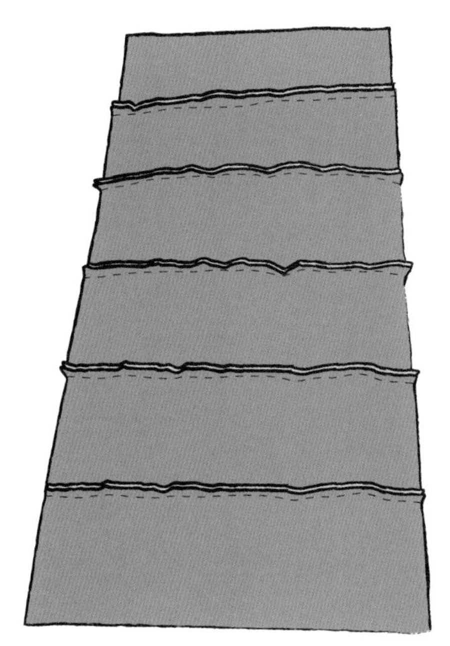

STEP 1

2 Press all selvedges of the seams to the right side. Flip the piece over to the right side and use your contrasting thread to topstitch ⅛" directly to the left of the seam. This strengthens each seam, keeps the selvedge/seam allowance tidy, and adds sophistication to the outside of the bag. A zipper foot works wonderfully to guide the needle straight down the seam, but it isn't necessary.

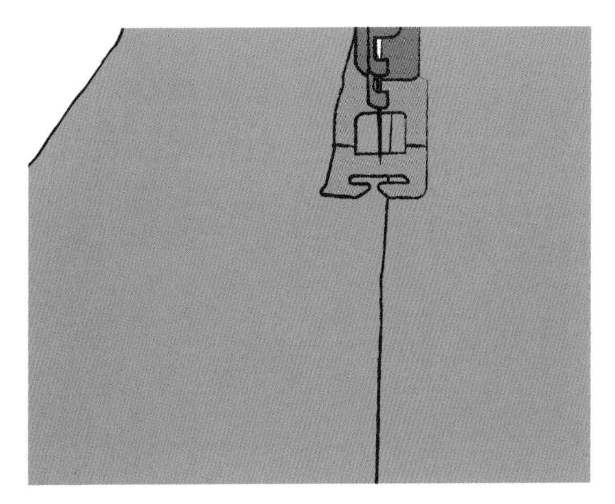

STEP 2

3 Repeat this topstitching for every seam to create two patch-worked pieces that measure approximately 10" × 22". Together these pieces are used for the main body of the bag.

STEP 3

4 Put it all together: Pin the 12" × 22" rectangle to one 22" edge of each patch-worked piece with the denim sides facing. Sew with ¼" seam allowance.

5 Press the seam allowances away from the patch-worked sides. Flip to the outside and topstitch ⅛" from the seam onto the bottom of the bag (not on the patch-worked pieces)

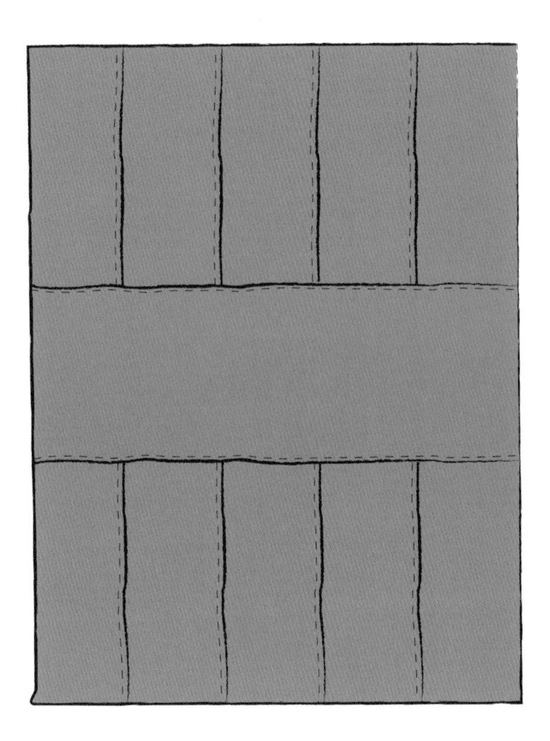

STEP 5

6 Place one top band (the 2" × 22" strips) along each loose edge of the patch-worked pieces with the denim sides facing. Sew using a ¼" seam allowance.

7 Press the seam allowance toward the band. Flip over and topstitch ⅛" from the seam directly onto the band. You have successfully created a large piece of fabric out of rescued jeans!

8 Fold the piece in half so that the edges with the top bands meet. The denim side should be on the outside and topstitched right sides are together. Pin the sides shut. Make sure to match the topstitched seams of the bottom and also match the bands on both sides. Sew the side edges shut with a ¼" seam allowance.

9 Box the corners of each side. To do this, take the top of each side seam and bring them together. You should have a diamond that intersects evenly in both directions.

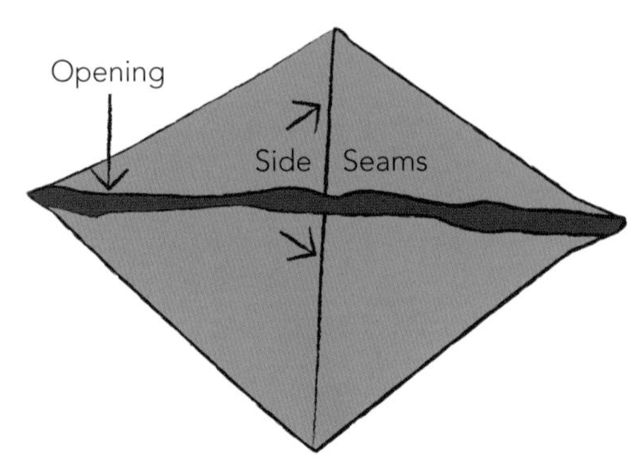

STEP 9

10 Using a ruler, draw a straight line across the seamed corners with tailor's chalk or a pen to create a triangle. Your line should measure 4" across. Pin on both sides of the line. Make sure that your lines are parallel with one another and that the opening forms another straight parallel line. Sew along the chalk lines, making sure to lock stitches. Trim off the excess fabric (snip the corner).

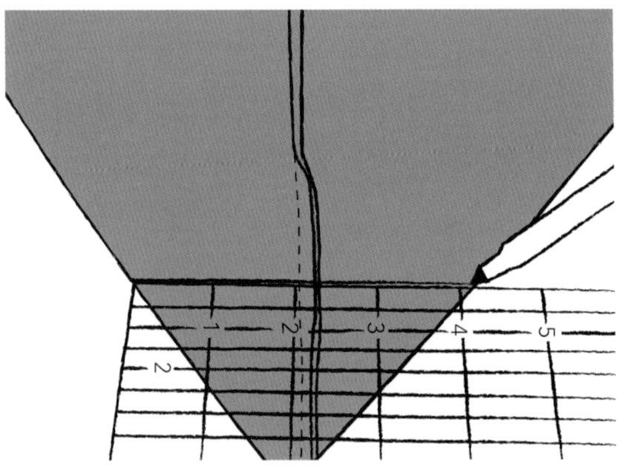

STEP 10

Create the Interior

1 Cut your pillow case or cotton to 22" × 43".

2 Fold the rectangle in half so the 22" edges are together and the right sides are facing. Pin the side seams and then sew them with ¼" seam allowance.

3 Box the corners in the same fashion as you did the exterior.

Insert the Interior Hang Pocket

This is a clever and practical way to hint at the true identity of the original fabric (blue jeans!) and tie the exterior and interior together.

1 Cut a piece of the same jeans into a 7½" × 19" rectangle.

2 With the denim side up, fold the bottom (short side) up ½" and press. Fold over ½" once more and press. Topstitch ¼" from the edge closest to the denim.

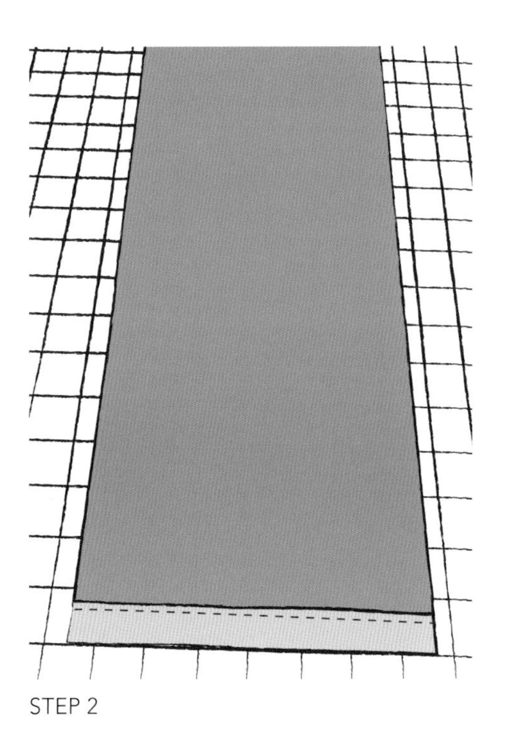

STEP 2

3 Flip the rectangle so that the denim side is face down and the hemmed is edge still at the bottom. Fold up the bottom side 6½" and pin in place. Set aside.

4 Cut two 2" × 13" strips of the interior lining fabric. Fold each in half lengthwise and press. Open and fold each end to the center crease mark. Press. Enclose the raw edges of the pocket sides with these strips and pin them in place. You should have a little extra fabric at the bottom to fold under. Stitch in place.

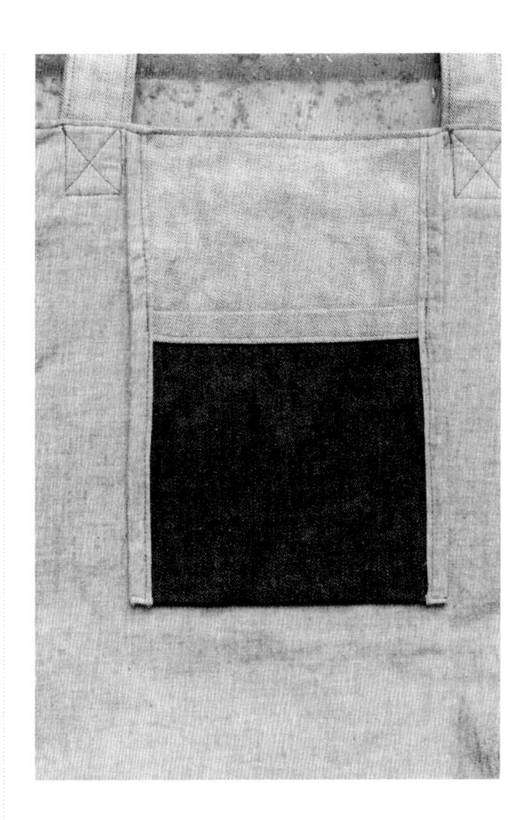

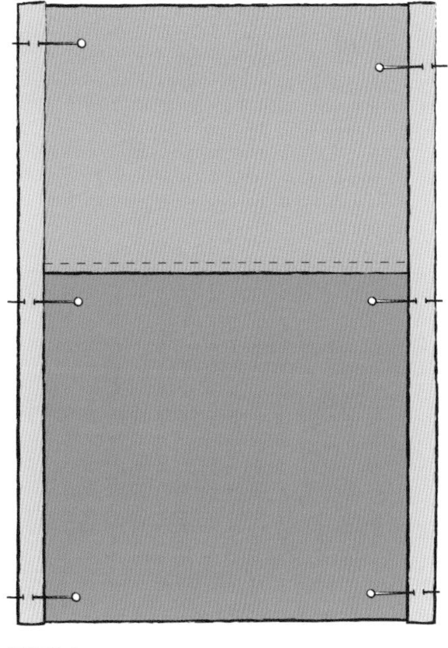

STEP 4

5 Attach the pocket to the interior. Find the center of the top edge of one side of the interior. Finger press it to create a crease. Do the same thing with the center of the top edge of the pocket. Match these two creases and pin the pocket in place. (The top of the pocket is flush with the top of the interior.) Baste along the top edge.

Put It All Together

1 Baste each handle to the top edge of the exterior portion of the bag. The handles' ends should extend 2" above the top edge of the bag. Position them equally distanced from the side seams of the bag and there should be 7¾" between them. The pocket should be positioned directly between them.

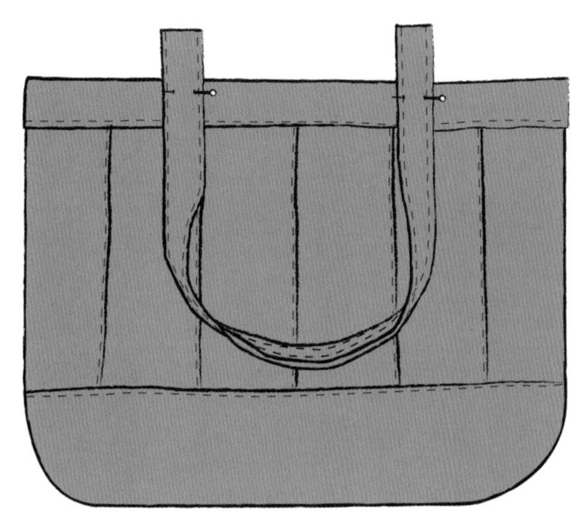

STEP 1

2 Turn the lining inside out so that the right side is on the inside. Insert the exterior bag and tuck in the handles. The right side of the interior should be touching the right side of the exterior. Sew along the top edge with a ¼" seam allowance, leaving 8" open on the side opposite the pocket.

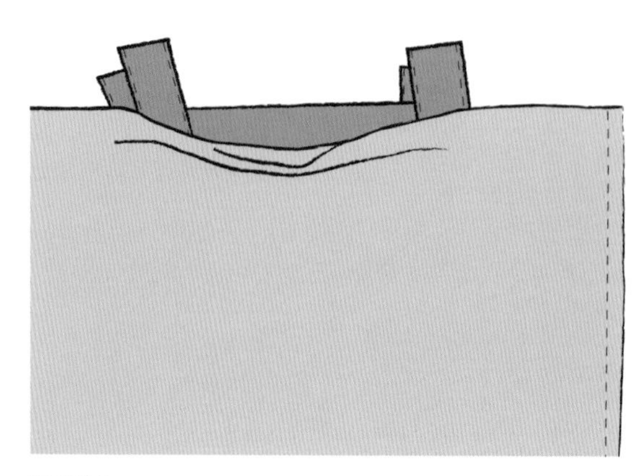

STEP 2

3 Turn the bag right side out through the opening and tuck the interior into the bag. Press and pin the opening shut. Topstitch the entire perimeter and close the opening. Create a boxed X over the end of each strap in the band portion of the bag. This reinforces the straps for heavy hauling. This bag is now ready to fill!

LITTLE RIVER RUG

LITTLE RIVER RUG

Finished Dimensions: 17" × 32"

The different shades of blue in this denim rug are outlined with a soft intentional fray, bringing to mind flowing water. The double zigzag pattern is the hieroglyph for the Nile River, as well as the symbol for the astrological sign of Aquarius, the water bearer. By creating this pattern with the triangle square, a traditional quilting method, it's also connected to the early 20th century quilts, where old work clothes and overalls were common sources for fabric. With all of this rug's symbolism, it can serve beautifully as a display piece, but it's durable enough to handle lots of foot traffic. Don't hesitate to place it on the floor—just throw it in the washing machine when it needs freshening. Make a larger custom size simply by adding more rows and squares.

NOTE: In these instructions, the reverse side of denim is named right side and the outside of the jeans is referred to as denim.

SUPPLIES

- Several pairs of jeans in both light and dark shades
- ½ yard of pre-washed heavy cotton canvas or twill
- Ruler
- Rotary cutter
- Cutting mat
- Pen

Make the Triangle Squares

1 Cut 16 5" squares of light denim and 16 5" squares of dark denim for a total of 32 squares.

2 Pair a light and dark square with the denim sides touching to make a total of 16 pairs of squares.

3 Using a ruler and pen, mark a straight line from one corner to another. Repeat this step with all 16 pairs.

4 Sew a parallel seam on both sides of the line. Place the presser foot on the edge of the line as your guide. To make fast work of this step, set all prepped squares next to your machine and sew down one side of each square without even lifting the presser foot. Just feed them continuously through, remembering to lock stitches. After the last one, turn and sew the other seam of each square.

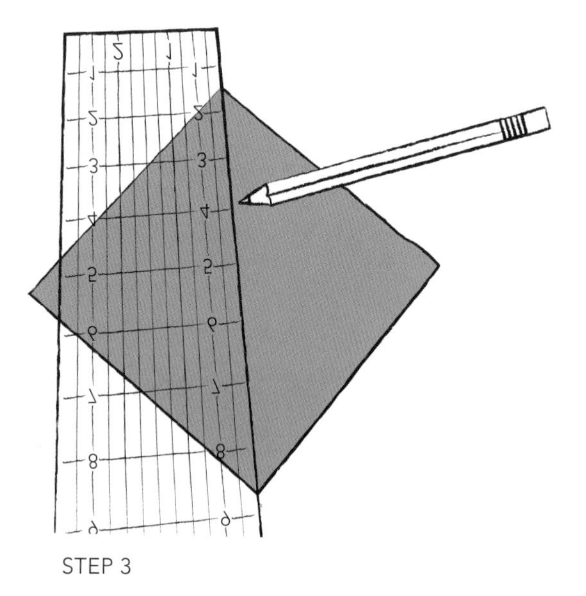

STEP 3

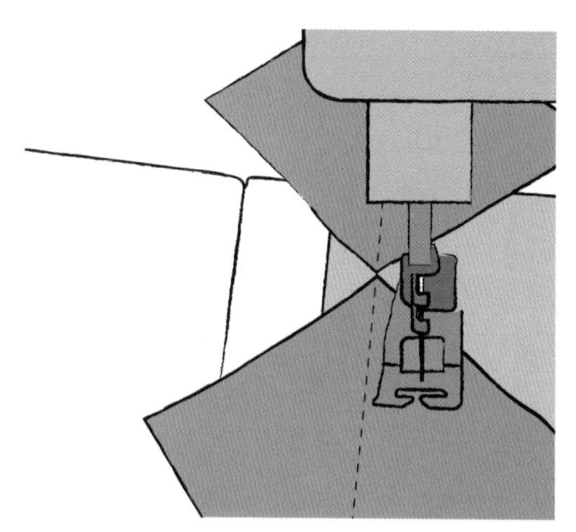

STEP 4

5 Detach each square by cutting the threads that connect them. Use scissors to cut straight along the penned line. You now have 32 triangles with a seam along one edge. Snip each corner at the end of the seam, being careful to not get too close to the stitches.

6 Open the triangle to reveal a square made of two contrasting halves. Press the seam open and flat. The side with the seam exposed is the right side. This selvedge becomes the frayed outline at the very end!

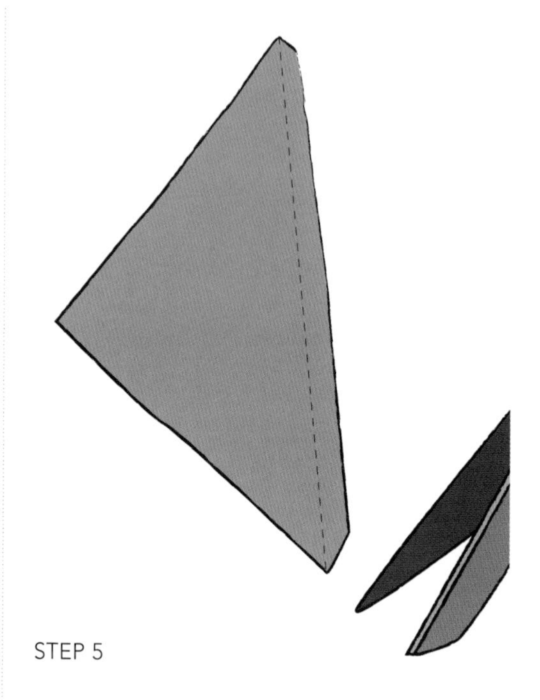

STEP 5

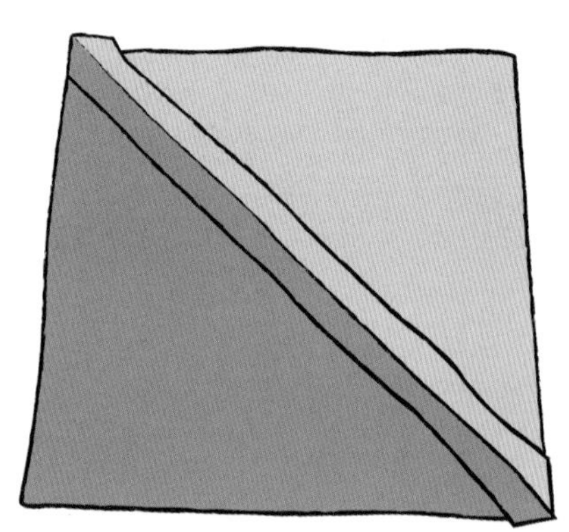

STEP 6

Arrange the Squares

The triangle squares are the basis for creating a plethora of patterns. Make sure to experiment and see the possibilities of new designs you could create for future rugs. For the Little River Rug, lay out two panels as shown in the illustration.

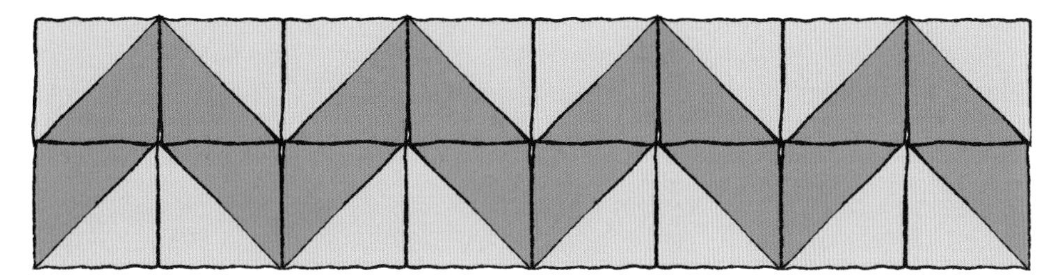

ARRANGING THE SQUARES FOR THE RUG

Sew the Squares into Strips

1 Sew long strips of eight squares together by laying one on top of another with right sides (the sides with the exposed seams) touching. Place the presser foot at the edge of the fabric and sew down the length of one square. Lock stitches. Make sure to face the squares in the direction of the pattern that you laid out and keep adding squares until all eight are sewn together in a row.

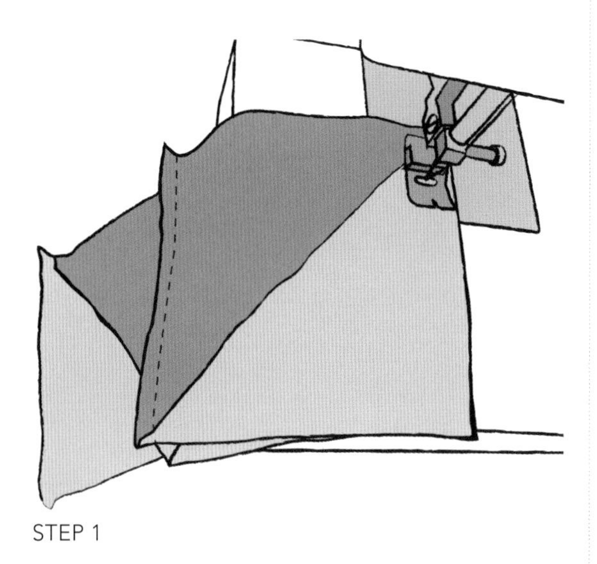

STEP 1

2 Repeat this process for all rows. Continue to be mindful of the pattern. You will have four long strips. Press open all seams that you have just sewn.

Connecting the Strips

1 Take rows and pair them so that you have a larger strip that has a dark zigzag pattern. Pin the strips together with right sides facing, taking care to match up all seams. Continue using the edge of the presser foot as your seam allowance, and stitch the first set together.

2 Repeat with the next set.

3 Pin the two sets together to create the center (paler) zigzag pattern. Once again, place right side to right side. Press all seams and bumpy cross points open to make them as flat as possible.

Create the Binding

1 Square up all of the sides. (Using a cutting mat with a grid, a ruler, and a rotary cutter is extremely helpful for this process.) Cut a rectangle the same size as the patch-worked mat out of sturdy cotton for the rug's backing.

2 Cut long 2"-wide strips of the dark denim. The total length of the binding needs to be approximately 102" long, but measure your mat to ensure that you have more than enough. Join strips as you would for making bias tape even though the strips may or may not be cut on the bias. Pin two strips, denim sides together, at a right angle to each other. Use a ruler to draw a 45° line. Sew along the line. Press the seam open and trim the excess seam allowance as well as any protruding corners. Join as many strips as needed for the required length of the rug perimeter.

3 Fold the binding strip in half widthwise and press down the entire length. Open and then fold the long edges toward the center crease. Press. Fold the strip in half so your folded edges meet and press.

4 Sandwich the two layers of one short side of the mat inside the binding strip. Do not pin the binding in place yet because it might shift when you create the corners. Pause frequently to make sure that you are catching both sides of the binding. Stitch to the end of the first edge. Wrap the binding around the corner and pin the next side in place. Tuck the corner edge into place and pin at the mitered fold. Resume stitching. Repeat this step for each corner.

5 Continue stitching in this manner until you reach the beginning of the binding. The end should overlap the beginning edge by 2". Tuck under the final ends and finish with locked stitches. Remove the pins from the corners and hand-stitch each corner with sturdy thread if necessary.

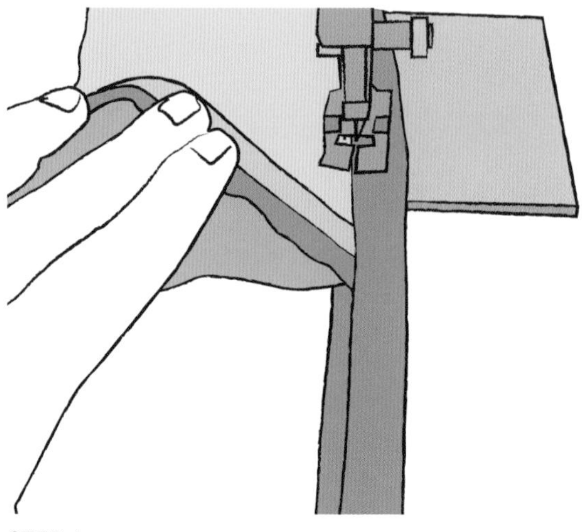

STEP 4

6 Toss the rug in the washing machine and dryer to encourage the frayed outline. Done!

HAMMOCK HIDEAWAY

HAMMOCK HIDEAWAY

Finished Dimensions: approximately 56" × 110"

Who doesn't long for a lazy day swaying in the shade of a tree? Combining the softness of a sheet with the durability of denim, this hammock is the ultimate summer day bed. Its unique shape creates a roomy nest for relaxing, as well as offering protective sides that ward off insects or evening chills. Safety and security were factored in with double and triple seams, plus jute webbing at the major stress points. This is a wonderful weekend project that will get constant use from the moment it's completed.

SUPPLIES

- 4 or more pairs of large jeans
- 4–5 yards of jute upholstery webbing
- 2 yards of heavy cotton (denim, painter's cloth, canvas, etc.)
- 1 large bed sheet (double or larger)
- Strong, thick rope that states it can hold 300 pounds or more
- Two large steel hooks
- A bit of adventure

Cutting the Jeans

Because all jeans are different sizes and shapes these instructions are more like guidelines than an exact recipe. This hammock utilizes the shape of pant legs to create a perfect cradle for your body. When you open up the side of one leg you can see the extra fabric usually cut on the bias that's added at the thigh area. Cut off the bottom hem of each leg and as far up to the back pocket as possible. Open up the leg on the seam that is not topstitched. This is almost always the outer seam. This hammock also calls for straight, rectangular panels, which you create from only one side of a pant leg. Rip up the leg to find a straight edge on the grain line.

1 Cut out five pant legs and open them. Create at least eight straight panels, as well.

2 Arrange these pieces using the chart for inspiration about placement and direction. Feel free to create your own combination, too!

3 There will be three rows of denim pieces. Sew the pieces of the rows together first. Press the seams to one side and then turn the piece over to the right side. Topstitch close to the seam edge and on top of the seam allowance beneath for every piece. These double seams are important, so please don't skip this step.

4 Trim the rows to make them even before you stitch them together.

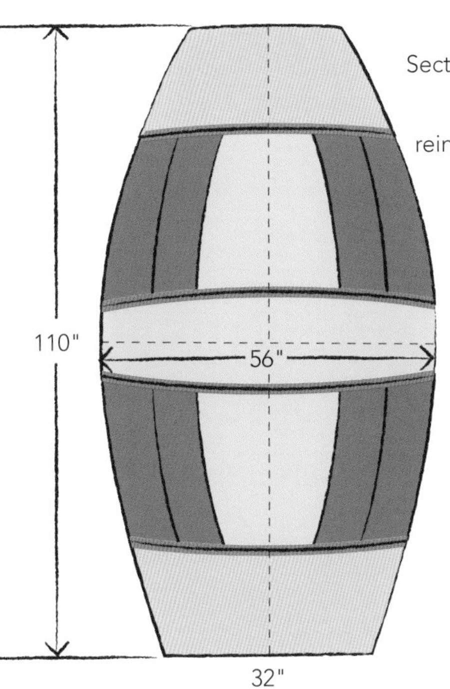

HAMMOCK LAYOUT EXAMPLE

5 Refer to the chart for inspiration of how to add more yardage of a strong fabric on either end.

6 Pin jute webbing directly over all the seams that run across the width. Sew both sides of the jute webbing down. The sample hammock has a total of four strips of jute webbing.

7 Place the denim side of the hammock on top of a sheet with the right sides facing. Use the hammock exterior as a template for cutting out the sheet. Pin together and sew around the perimeter leaving an opening for turning at one of the ends.

8 Turn the hammock right side out. Press the opening closed and pin. Sew around the entire edge of the hammock.

9 Fold over each (hanging) end about 7" onto the sheet side of the hammock. Pin and then sew three parallel seams across it to keep it in place and make it super strong.

10 Push a strong and resilient rope through the channel and knot it. Hang the hammock from two sturdy hooks. Grab some lemonade and enjoy!

Hamaca

I've always loved hammocks, and I have quite a vivid memory of my first hammock experience. It was 1974. I was five years old. My mother and I had an adventure with her best friend, who had a child just my age. We all took a train and bus trip down to Mexico. A last-minute change in itinerary landed the four of us in a remote, and yet to be discovered, fishing village. Unbeknownst to us, hotels had not yet come to little Santa Cruz. Transportation was sporadic, and we were temporarily stranded. Fortunately, a kind family took us under their wing and let us stay in their empty palapa (thatched hut) on the beach. Saying it was unfurnished is an understatement. Its only amenity was the soft sand floor. The father and brother went up to the mountains to harvest some trees to make two frames for hanging woven rope beds. I might have been small, but I still remember the feeling of the rope cradling me as I swayed to sleep in my mother's arms in that Mexican hamaca. We came home to the States with a hammock in hand. Onto our back porch it went, a colorful woven reminder of a mother-daughter adventure. ■

CHAPTER 8

MAILERS

Dupont™ Tyvek® is a light-weight, water- and tear-resistant material made from flashspun high-density polyethelene fibers. Resembling a cross between paper and cloth, its unique properties lend itself to a multitude of uses from house siding to clothing, yet it is most recognizable as an ordinary mailing envelope. Tyvek mailers join the ranks of other plastics that aren't easily recycled, including billboards, grocery bags, and event banners. It is a post-industrial material ripe with possibilities for repurposing.

History

Tyvek was discovered by a DuPont researcher in the 1950s and was introduced commercially ten years later. Its first uses were for light-weight and water-resistant fabric often utilized in the medical industry for disposable garments and packaging sterile supplies. Its soft drape must have inspired 1970s powerhouse designer Fiorucci, who created an entire Tyvek line. The next decade was to be the most important in Tyvek's short history. In the 1980s Tyvek gained popularity in the building industry when it was introduced as protective covering for houses. This remains one of Tyvek's main uses even today. However, artists and crafters are continuing to find new and innovative ways to work with its interesting properties.

Sourcing

Tyvek is easily found in your mailbox. Ask friends to save their mailers for you, and soon you'll have a nice stash to work with.

Deconstructing

- Cut open two sides of a standard mailer envelope to access the interior. Make sure to use the scissors you've designated for paper, as the plastic in Tyvek will dull the blades of fabric shears. This is all that is needed to create a usable piece of material for sewing.
- Sew or glue together several pieces to create a larger piece.

Tips

- Choose to embellish either one or both sides with paints or printing. I like to leave a few reminders of its former life as a mailer so that its reinvention efforts are not forgotten.
- You can enhance the plastic fibers by applying a thick coat of acrylic craft paint. Before it dries, wipe away the excess paint with a rag. The result is a wonderful textured surface that resembles the patina of worn leather or canvas.
- Stamping on Tyvek requires the use of a solvent ink pad so that it doesn't smear. Look at most craft stores for ink designed especially for use on plastic or laminated paper.
- Permanent markers work beautifully on the surface of Tyvek, but you need to protect your work surface because the ink bleeds to the other side.
- Keep Tyvek away from hot irons as it is plastic and melts.
- Try to avoid ripping out seams in Tyvek. The holes made by a needle are permanent.

Environmental Impact

Tyvek is a petroleum-based plastic. It has been included in this book not to encourage crafting with new, nor the production of more, Tyvek but to showcase the potential of reusing what has already been manufactured. Because Tyvek mailers are not a standard recyclable material, the only option is to send them directly back to their manufacturer, DuPont. A creative and green alternative is to reinvent the mailers you receive so that their story doesn't abruptly end with a single use.

COLOR BLOCK ZIPPERED POUCH

COLOR BLOCK ZIPPERED POUCH

Finished Dimensions: 6½" × 8"

Make your own recycled "fabric" in the color palette of your choice and patchwork it together for a totally unique catch-all. Slip in a zipper and you're ready to fill it with all of your small essentials. Zippers often bring up sewing insecurities, but they are surprisingly easy to insert. This pouch is a perfect first zipper experience—straightforward, painless, and quick. The end result is a modern accessory and a feeling of confidence.

SUPPLIES

Tyvek mailer
Craft knife and cutting mat
Ruler
Acrylic paint or fabric paint
Rag
Paint brush
9" zipper
1½" twill tape (optional)

Prepare the Tyvek

Painting Tyvek with acrylics or decorating it with permanent markers transforms this basic material into a one-of-a-kind piece.

1 Open the mailer with paper scissors and paint each side a different color. Wipe off any excess paint with a rag. Let dry.

2 From one color cut two 3" × 9" pieces and from the other color cut two 5" × 9" pieces.

3 Place two contrasting pieces together with the right sides facing (the painted sides are the right sides). Align the two pieces along one of the 9" sides and then sew along the side with a ⅜" seam allowance.

4 Open the seam and finger press it toward the larger piece.

STEPS 3 AND 4

Make the Pouch

1 Attach the zipper foot to your sewing machine. Your sewing machine manual will instruct you how to do this. It's very straightforward.

2 Line up the top edge of the zipper (face down) with the top edge of the Tyvek's right side. Do not pin in place as this will leave permanent holes in the Tyvek.

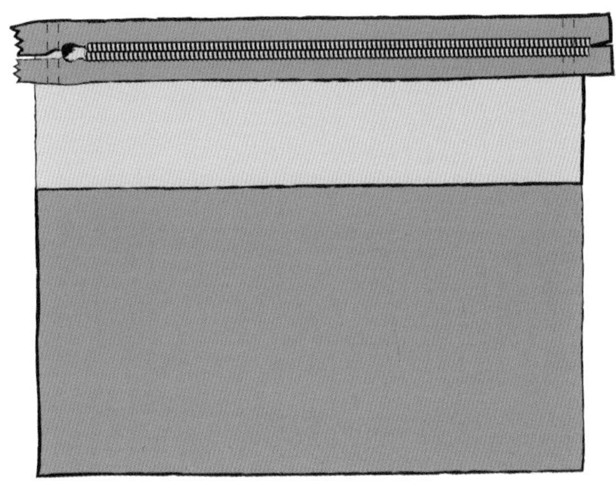

STEP 2

3 Sew along the side of the zipper as close to the edge as possible. You might have to pause to move the zipper out of the way in order to keep the seam straight; simply keep the needle down, but lift the foot up and then slip the zipper past the area being sewn before putting the foot back down again. Resume sewing.

4 Repeat Steps 2 and 3 with the opposite side of the zipper and the second piece of Tyvek. Turn right side out and top stitch the Tyvek directly where it meets the zipper on both sides. This gives it a polished and finished look, but it also reinforces the zipper.

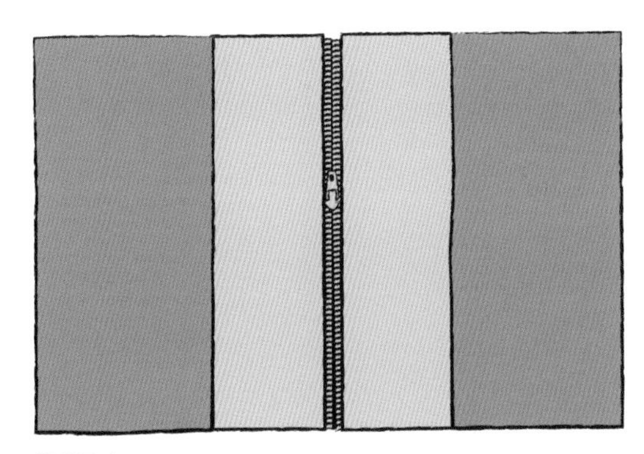

STEP 4

5 Turn inside out and unzip the zipper at least ¾ of the way. This is a very important step. Fold in half with right sides together with the zipper at the top.

6 Starting at the top of one side, sew all three open sides with a ¼" seam allowance. Make sure to backstitch at the beginning and end.

7 For a nice mix of materials you might want to insert a twill tape loop before sewing. Do this without pinning, just hold it in place until the seam reaches it.

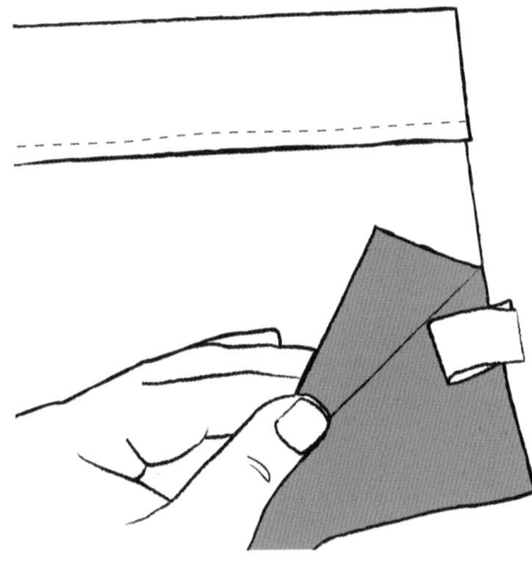

STEP 7

8 Snip off the corners. Turn the pouch right side out through the unzipped slot.

9 That's it! The pouch is ready to fill with all of your sewing supplies or little odds and ends that are floating to the bottom of your bag. You can never have too many pouches!

BANNER

BANNER

Finished Dimensions: Customizable

This colorful banner adds an instant festive element to any location at next to no cost and with very little effort. A small banner is wonderful for a child's party or coordinated to a bedroom's décor. Because Tyvek is made to handle weather, the banners also make fantastic decorations for outdoor parties and are quite at home all summer long in the garden. The only limit to size and shape is your stash of Tyvek.

SUPPLIES

- Tyvek mailer
- Banner template (choose your own size and shape and make a template on cardstock)
- Acrylic paint
- Brush
- Rag
- Craft knife and cutting mat
- Ruler
- Ribbon if the banner will be hung outside

NOTE: The sample banner was made with a triangle measuring 3" across and 4" long.

Paint the Tyvek

1 Cut out at least a dozen banner triangles using your ruler, craft knife, and cutting mat.

2 Paint each side and immediately wipe off all excess paint with a rag. Let dry.

3 Lay out a pattern of colors and then stack them up with the first on top.

Sew the Banner

1 Set the sewing machine to a larger zigzig stitch, such as 4mm.

2 Pull at least 12" of thread/bobbin out before you begin sewing. This extra thread provides the tail for hanging the banner.

3 Sew along the top of the right side of the first triangle near the edge. Do not backstitch when you come to the end.

4 Keep sewing (through air) and gently pulling the triangle so that there is about an inch of thread between the first triangle and the next.

5 Add the next triangle in the same fashion as the first. Repeat until you have sewn all the triangles into the banner. End by pulling enough thread to hang on the other side (12" once again).

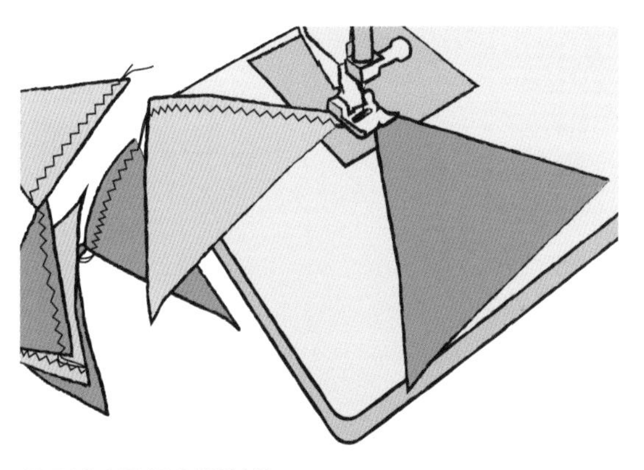

STEPS 3 THROUGH 5

6 Your banner is ready to be hung in honor of someone or something special!

Variation for Outdoors

1 If you'd like a sturdier banner or want to hang it outside, sew triangles to a length of ribbon.

2 With this method, choose if you'd like the ribbon to be on the front or the back of the banner. Using a ribbon that's lovely on both sides ensures that the banner can be reversible.

3 Sew each triangle directly to the ribbon with a straight or decorative stitch. Space the triangles ¾" apart.

Celebrating Vintage Educational Toys

The wooden people that line the wall on the barn shelf are the same ones I played with as a child in my grandparents' home. My grandfather was a physicist and an inventor. My grandmother was a graduate of the Bank Street College of Education and had been trained by the leaders of the progressive education movement. Together they built the first passive solar-heated house on Long Island in 1948. A few years later they added an addition—a cooperative nursery school for my grandmother to teach in and direct. This was my first home and the most constant house during my nomadic childhood.

During the summers I had the nursery school all to myself . . . it was any child's dream. My grandmother understood the importance of play fostered by open-ended materials. Every corner of her nursery school reflected her philosophy and inspired the parenting choices I make today. When seeking toys for my own children I am attracted to the classic educational toys I grew up with. I keep these words in mind:

> *The selection of play materials should never be haphazard or casual. A good toy leaves room for the free exercise of a child's imagination and can be used in many different ways. It is handsome in shape and color, is good to touch, beautiful in line, and interesting in texture. It is sturdy and will take heavy use. A good toy will fit into various play settings as dictated by a child's fancies. It quickens curiosity and invention as it lets the child find things out for herself.*
>
> ~ THERESA AND FRANK CAPLAN, CO-FOUNDERS OF CREATIVE PLAYTHINGS AND AUTHORS OF MANY BOOKS ON EARLY CHILDHOOD EDUCATION.

If play is the work of childhood, toys are the tools of their trade.

NOTEBOOK

NOTEBOOK

Finished Dimensions: 4" × 6½"

Making your own notebooks couldn't be easier and more satisfying. Keep your lists and inspiration on hand with pocket-sized books. These basic instructions will transfer to any other dimensions desired, so customize them to suit your needs. A notebook slipped into the linen portfolio from Chapter 3 would make a wonderful gift for young and old alike.

SUPPLIES

- 2 6½" × 8" rectangles of Tyvek
- 8 sheets of paper (printer or other found paper) cut slightly smaller than the Tyvek (use more if your machine is sturdy)
- Acrylic paint
- Brush
- Rag
- Square of linen with stenciled or stamped image (sized to fit the cover)
- Craft knife
- Cutting mat
- Ruler
- Paper cutter (optional, but helpful for slicing paper to size)

Paint the Tyvek

1 Place both rectangles together. Sew around the perimeter ⅛" from the edge.

2 Paint each side and immediately wipe off all excess with a rag. Let dry.

Attach the Cover

NOTE: These steps start with instructions to add an optional stenciled linen detail to your Tyvek cover. If you don't want to include this detail, start with Step 3.

1 Pull threads off of each side of the linen scrap to reveal the raw edged fringe. Straighten the edges with a rotary cutter.

2 Apply a stencil or stamp on a word—or both. Dry and heat set.

3 Fold the cover in half. Attach the linen piece to the center of the front of the notebook with straight stitching around the perimeter.

4 Fold the interior papers in half and make a sharp crease.

5 Insert the crease of the paper into the fold of the cover.

6 Set your sewing machine to a 5mm stitch length and sew straight down the crease. Make sure to secure the first and last stitches with a backstitch.

7 Paint the binding thread on the outside of the cover to match the cover color. Wipe away excess. It's hard to resist making a notebook for every occasion!

LUGGAGE TAGS

LUGGAGE TAGS

Finished Dimensions: 5" × 3¼"

The indestructible nature of Tyvek makes it the perfect material for crafting one-of-a-kind luggage tags. You'll spot your suitcase instantly in a crowd with a unique tag that can stand up to some pretty rugged terrain, as well as the elements.

Make the Tag

1 Trace template onto a Tyvek envelope and cut out two for each tag.

2 Choose a paint color and apply it to one side of each Tyvek rectangle. Quickly wipe away the excess paint with a rag before it dries. Use permanent markers to add identification info to one side and decorate the other. I used a manual typewriter to type an address onto a smaller piece of Tyvek in a contrasting color and then I stitched it in place to one side of the luggage tag.

3 Fold the elastic in half and sandwich it between the two tag pieces at the center of the angled top.

4 Sew around the entire perimeter of the tag. Backstitch back and forth over the elastic to secure it in place.

5 Loop the tag around the handle of your suitcase and you're ready to roam!

SUPPLIES

- Two rectangles of Tyvek (use the luggage tag template on page 182)
- Extra scraps of Tyvek for optional embellishment
- Acrylic paint and paint brushes
- Rag
- Permanent markers
- 7" of ½" elastic

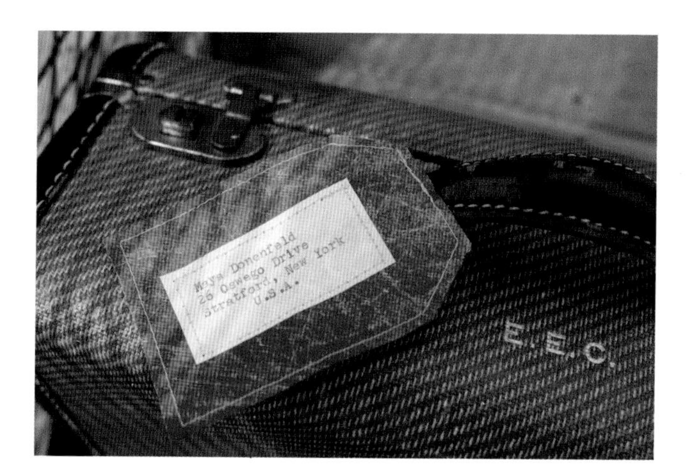

CHAPTER 9

VINTAGE

Textiles that have weathered the test of time remain the nostalgic remnants and reminders of a much simpler era. Incorporating these materials into our sewing connects us to our collective past; a woven bridge between yesterday and today. Home textiles are inherently intimate, reflecting the lives of those who used them. The souls of the women who came before us remain stitched into the seams of the aprons they wore and the fibers of the tablecloths they fed their family upon. Whether we inherit our own family heirlooms or rescue found ones, the act of honoring those humble homemakers is as compelling as the designs and motifs printed on the fabric.

History

The roles of women and home textiles are closely aligned and each era has had its own distinct style. From the lace tatting of the Victorian times to the vibrant and bold patterns of the mid 20th century, social history has been woven into the fabric of each piece. Until the mid '60s, gender roles were clearly defined and the domestic arts were not only a woman's domain but an expression of her creativity. In the '70s and '80s, women left the home to join the work force, and the emphasis on homemaking shifted. Many put away their sewing machines and tablecloths. With the birth of the information age came not only an acceleration of the pace of life, but a yearning to slow it down. Vintage fabrics and a renewed interest in sewing signify the slower rhythm that we are trying to reclaim.

Sourcing

An abundance of older linens are waiting to be rescued at antique shops, thrift stores, yard sales, flea markets, auctions, eBay, and Etsy. Larger pieces such as tablecloths, curtains, and bedding offer the most yardage and are particularly suitable for projects that call for sizeable pieces. Also desirable are aprons, tea towels, pillow cases, lace trims, and notions. Look for strong and sturdy fibers for projects that need to be durable, but don't dismiss the fragility in some more delicate pieces; just find gentle ways to use them.

Deconstruction

- Because home textiles often come in rectangles, squares, and circles, they are ready for cutting and sewing after they have been laundered and pressed.
- Stains and holes are part of each piece's story. You can choose to mend, patch, stencil, or even highlight them as a design element.

Tips

- Most people recommend hand-washing vintage fabrics, however I throw all of the cotton and linen pieces directly into the washing machine and hang them on the line to dry. This is my test to see if they can hold up to everyday wear and tear.
- Geometric borders and repeated floral patterns are common in tablecloths and bed spreads. Hang these large pieces on a wall or clothesline to gain perspective on how to best utilize the prints in your project.

Environmental Impact

Consumerism encourages us to always buy new, but there are plenty of gently used home textiles, vintage or otherwise, waiting to be recycled. Some may be perfect for your next sewing project; others might serve beautifully as their intended use.

FOLD AND TIE CASE

FOLD AND TIE CASE

Finished Dimensions: approximately 8" × 11" when closed

This super quick project calls for the use of a tea towel. It utilizes the existing finished hems for a design that needs no cutting and minimal sewing. It's a perfect last-minute gift, or you can even whip one up as you pack for your next weekend trip. A little fold here and there with the addition of three straight seams and you're done. Instant sewing gratification! These cases are ideal for holding your underthings in a suitcase, but their many pockets make it a practical organizer for anywhere you want a little order—from your sewing basket to a diaper bag. Note: If you don't have a tea towel, you can substitute any sturdy cotton, but you need to hem the edges prior to making the case. I used a section of vintage coverlet for the sample case.

SUPPLIES

- 1 tea towel or hemmed cotton fabric piece measuring approximately 32" × 16", but a little larger works well, too
- 4 strips of twill tape or ribbon: 2 12" strips, 1 10" strip, and 1 4" strip
- Thread
- Pins
- Iron

Fold and Sew Case

1 Press the towel with your iron. Fold the towel in half lengthwise and press again.

NOTE: If you're not using a tea towel, hem the fabric on all four sides.

STEP 1

2 Open the towel and fold each short end toward the center crease mark. Leave a 1" gap between the two ends in the center. Press.

3 Fold the bottom edge directly toward the center widthwise. Make sure each fold and seam is lined up and pin in place. Press again.

4 Pin the 12" twill tape strips so that 1" is sandwiched between the folded-up side and the body of the case. The top edge of the tape should be flush with the edge of the folded-up side as shown in the illustration. Pin the 10" twill tape strip on the left side of the case. Find the center point of the left side. Pin one side of the 10" twill tape ½" from this center and the other side ½" in the other direction. Repeat this process with the 4" strip on the right side.

5 Sew around the entire perimeter ¼" from the edge. Make sure to stitch back and forth several times over each piece of twill tape.

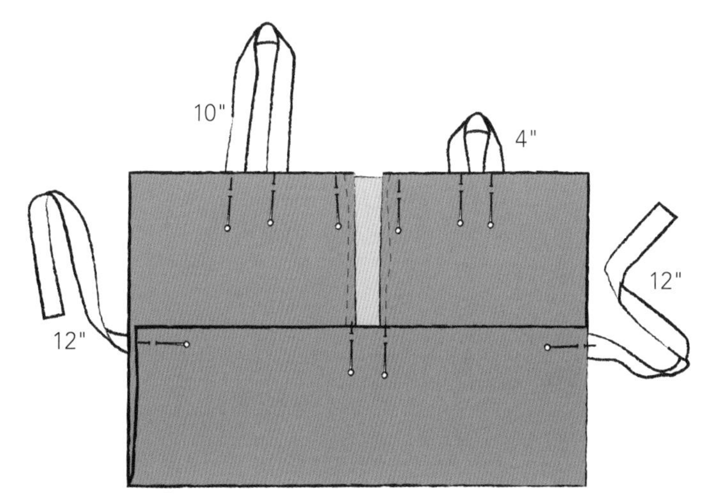

STEPS 3 AND 4

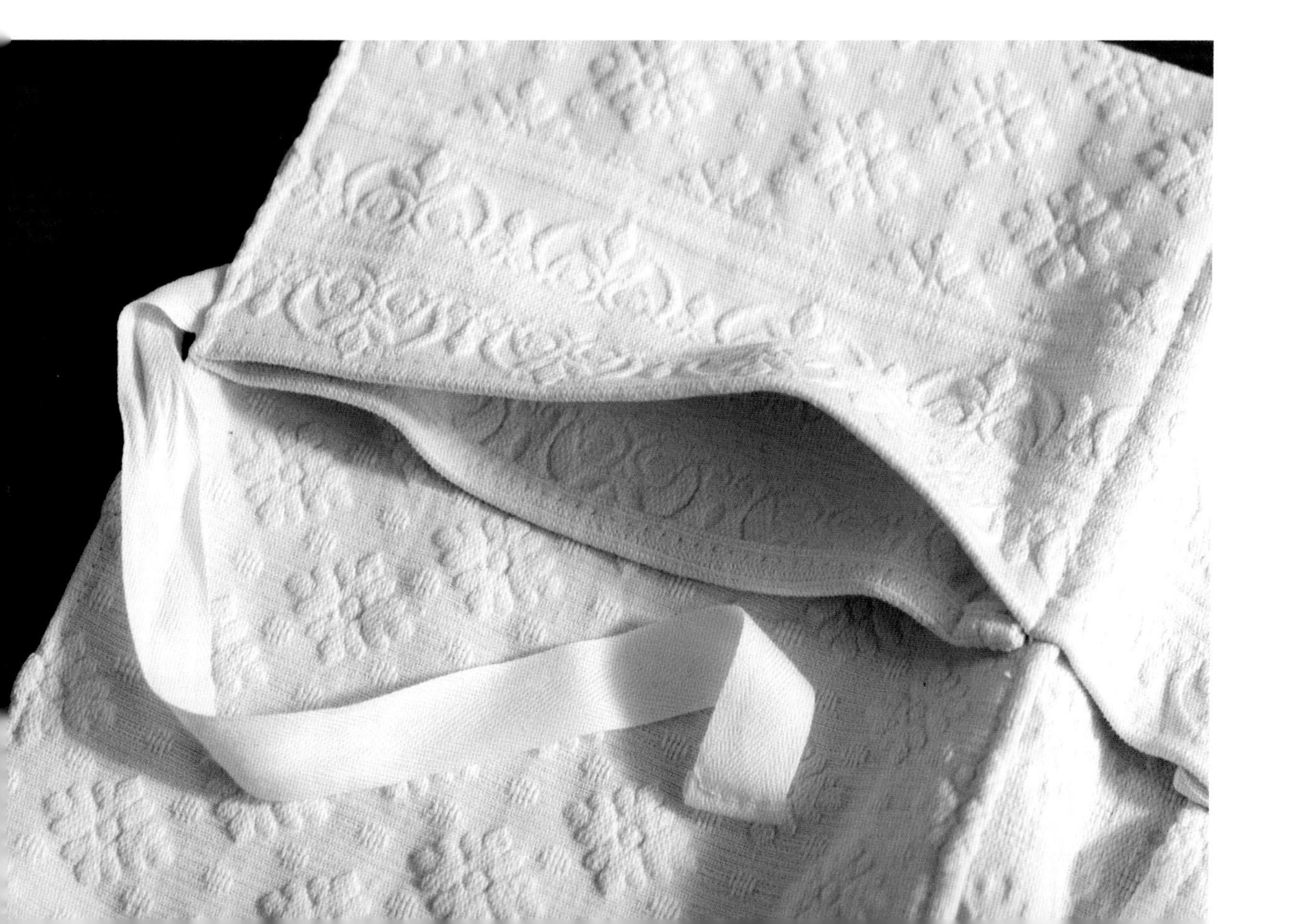

6 Sew up the two center seams, being careful to stop at the midpoint and backstitch. Finish the raw edges of the twill tape ties. Fold over twice ⅛". Press and stitch.

7 After filling the case with your essentials, tie it shut at the center with a bow. To "lock" the top in place and create a handy hanging loop, slip the longer loop into the shorter loop and hang from a knob or hook.

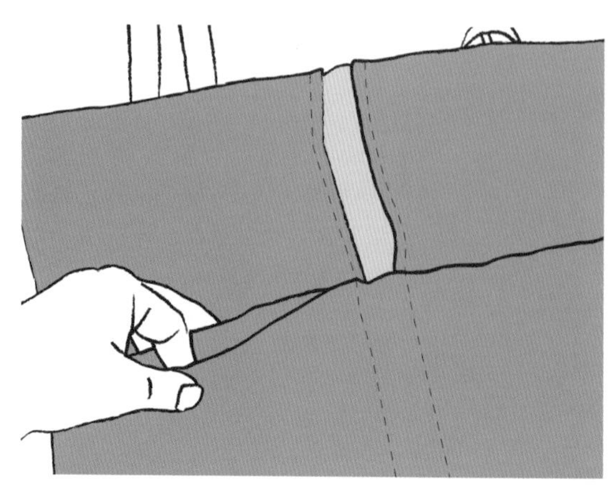

STEP 6

APRON BLOUSE

APRON BLOUSE

Finished dimensions: Customizable

What do you get when you sew two vintage half aprons together? A perfect little smock for doing chores, making art, or just adding a bit of whimsy to your wardrobe. In the '30s and '40s aprons were popular for their function as well as for their style. You can find them in abundance wherever vintage linens are for sale: flea markets, tag sales, etc. This quick project comes together in minutes and no pattern is needed!

SUPPLIES

- 2 half aprons that are similar in size and color scheme
- ¼" elastic

Assemble the Blouse

1 The waist of each apron morphs into the neckline and the waist ties become the shoulder ties! Place each apron right side down on your work surface. Fold a waist tie toward the center. Pin. Next fold the tie straight up.

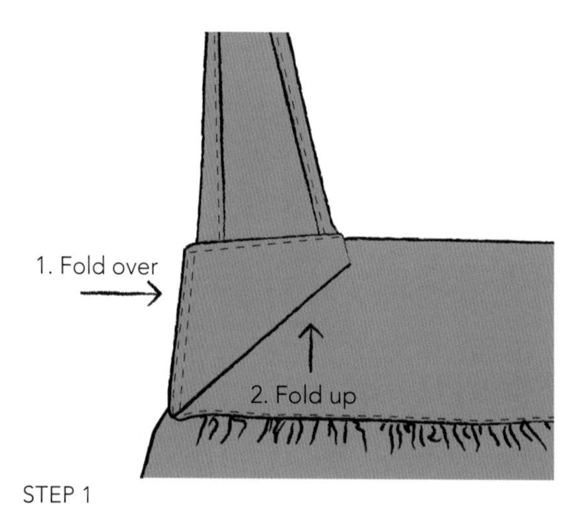

STEP 1

2 Stitch along the side and the new neckline. Repeat Steps 1 and 2 for each tie on both aprons.

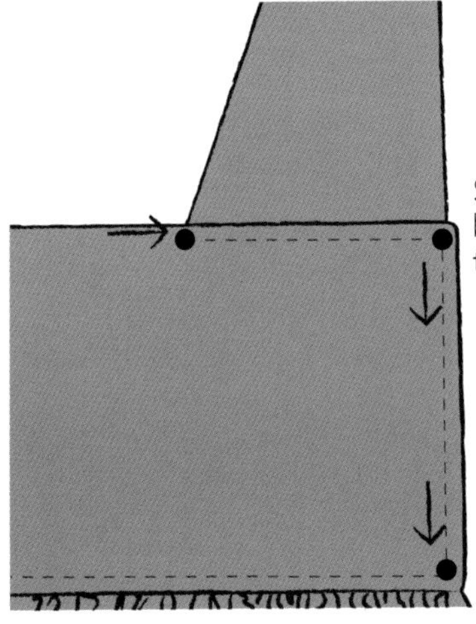

STEP 2

3 Lay the aprons one on top of the other with the right sides facing and sew up the sides, leaving several inches open under the arm. Try on for fit.

4 Measure the new neck line (what was the original waist). Divide by 2. This is how long each piece of elastic should be. Cut the elastic. Pin the center of the elastic to the center of the neckline ¼" from the edge. Pin each end to each side so that you have the elastic pinned in three places.

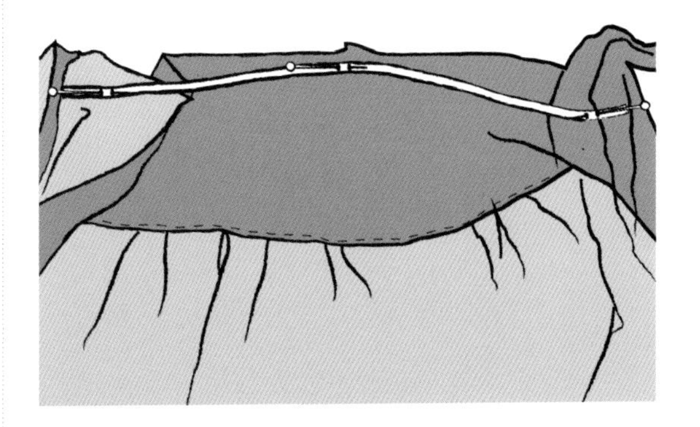

5 Beginning on one side, sew directly on the elastic, stretching it to lie flat against the apron. Pause at the center, remove the pin, and continue stretching and sewing. This will create a nice gather.

6 Tie the shoulder straps together. Done! You've just merged two humble pieces into one very clever new top!

SUMMER BOLSTER

SUMMER BOLSTER

Finished Dimensions: A square 40" table cloth holds a single or double comforter

When the warm months arrive, transform your winter down comforter into a plush summer bolster. The bolster doubles as welcome storage that's attractive enough to be out on display, and it makes a fabulous pillow for reading in bed or lounging on in the hammock. What a wonderful solution when space is at a premium! This bolster is a great way to display a favorite piece of vintage fabric; just make sure it's sturdy enough to handle the stress when you stuff the blanket inside. (Some older textiles can be too brittle and fragile for everyday use, while others are quite sturdy.) Larger pieces of antique textiles come in the form of bed sheets, coverlets, and tablecloths. They are easy to track down at flea markets and offer a wealth of different styles to choose from.

Make the Bolster

1 Fold the fabric in half with the right sides facing. Sew the long side opposite the fold with a ½" seam allowance. Press the seams open and stitch both sides down with a small zigzag stitch.

SUPPLIES

- 40" × 40" piece of fabric
- 2 yards of twill tape or ribbon
- Seam ripper
- Thread
- Pins
- Iron

STEP 1A

STEP 1B

2 Create a drawstring channel on both open ends by folding the fabric over 2" and pressing. Fold 2" a second time and press again. Sew in place at the bottom of the fold and stitch a second seam 1" from the top edge of the fold. Topstitch the edge, as well.

3 Turn the piece right side out. Use your seam ripper to open the seam in the drawstring channel. Stitch back and forth several times below and above the opening to reinforce the opening. Do this for both channels.

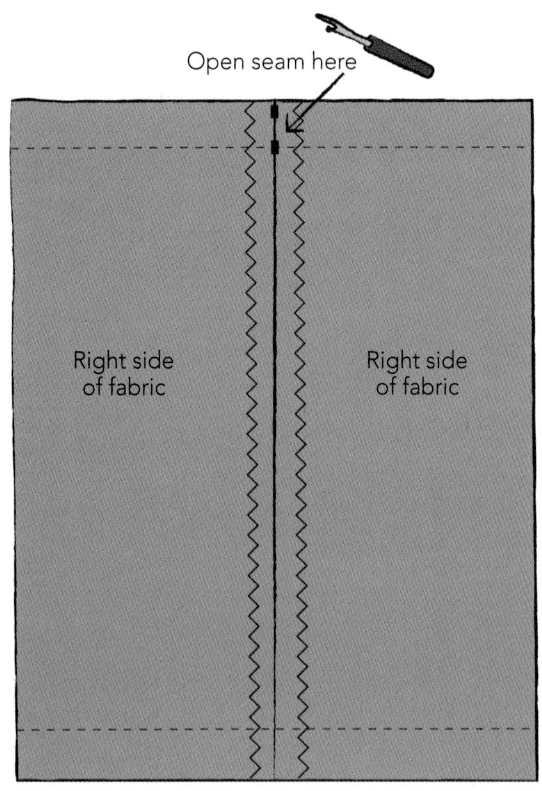

STEP 3

4 Thread the ribbon or twill tape through the channels with a safety pin. Fold the raw ends of the ribbon or tape over twice and stitch to finish the ends.

5 Cinch one side shut and tie with a bow. Stuff your comforter into the open side and cinch and tie it, as well. Toss this fluffy pillow onto your bed, grab a good read, and settle in for pure comfort and relaxation.

NOTE: Instead of using an old textile, you can create interest with any favortie fabric on hand. See the techniques in Chapters 1 and 2 for full instructions on how to

- Add several rows of tiny raw-edged ruffles several inches below and parallel to the drawstring channels
- Incorporate pencil pleats in any direction desired
- Stencil a printed pattern on solid fabric

The Dyne

As a small child, I stayed with my grandparents frequently. I slept in the tiny postage-stamp bedroom next to the stairs. My grandfather had been inspired by the boats he'd sailed upon when he built the house and utilized every available inch. Above my bed was a sliding wooden panel that accessed a small storage cabinet built into the slant above the stairwell. It was the perfect size for storing blankets when they weren't in use. I used to slide the panel open and crawl in to snuggle like a gosling among three big goose-down comforters that my grandmother affectionately referred to as "dynes" (pronounced doona). Years earlier, my grandparents had visited Europe and had taken a freighter home, laden with unconventional souvenirs—a trio of dynes. For decades my mother's family curled up under the warmth of goose feathers and sang the praise of these amazing Dutch blankets, a staple and tradition in many European countries. Today down comforters, cousins of the dyne, are available in every bedding store across the country and lay upon each bed in my home during our brutal East Coast winters. We don't have my grandparents' storage cabinet, so I designed this bolster as a space-saving solution for the modern home.

During the photo shoot at my mother's barn, I discovered that I had accidentally left behind my daughter's comforter, which the bolster had been created for. Cameras were in position, lighting was perfect, there was no time to race home. I desperately looked around the barn for something fluffy to use in its place. In a large basket, nestled beneath a stack of sheets, was one of my grandmother's dynes. It took my breath away, and I was instantly flooded with memories. I lovingly stuffed it into the bolster . . . a perfect fit. ■

TRAVELING HAMPER

TRAVELING HAMPER

Finished dimensions: 13" × 13" × 24"

You'll be happy to display your everyday storage when it features the bold prints of old textiles. This tall, upright hamper showcases the floral graphics found in vintage tablecloths as it stands waiting to be filled. Reminiscent of canvas tent construction, its dowel framework makes for lightweight portability, and it readily folds when not in use. Easily remove the dowels for occasional washing. The large size lends itself to versatility, so why limit it to the laundry room? Fill it with everything from soft toys to skeins of yarn, or make it the ultimate fabric scrap bin.

Make the Hamper

1 Cut four 26" × 13 ½" rectangles and one 13" square from both the tablecloth and the sheet.

2 Pin two 26" sides of the tablecloth together with right sides facing. Sew straight down the length using the edge of the presser foot as a guide for the seam allowance. Continue to sew all four rectangles together in this manner until they are all connected. When you're done, you should have an open-bottomed box of fabric. Press all seams out with an iron.

3 Pin the square to the bottom of the open-bottomed box, matching the corners to the seams of each rectangle. Continue to keep all right sides touching.

4 Repeat Steps 1 through 3 with the sheet.

Create the Dowel Channels

1 Make dowel slots in the lining. Use a water soluble pen or chalk to place two marks on each side seam 2" from the top and 3" from the top. Beginning at the 2" mark, sew a ¼" × 1" box with the seam at the center. Make sure to stitch back and forth several times at the top and bottom of the box where the marks are to lock the seam in place when it's opened. Open the seam within the box with a seam ripper. Give the same treatment to all four side seams in the lining.

SUPPLIES

- Sturdy tablecloth
- Bed sheet or something comparable for the hamper's lining
- 32" piece of 1 ½" twill tape or ribbon
- 4 ½" × 36" dowels
- Hand saw
- Sandpaper
- Safety pin
- Water soluble pen or chalk
- 11" × 11" piece of cardboard

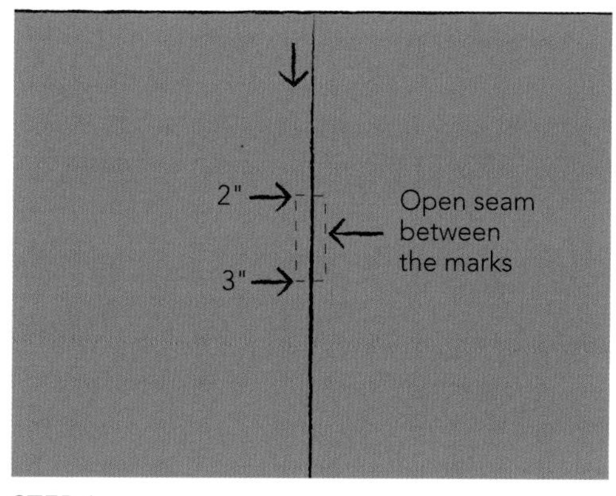

STEP 1

2 Turn the exterior right side out and slip it into the lining. The right sides of the exterior and the lining are now touching. Match each of the four side seams and pin the lining and the exterior together.

3 Cut eight 3 ½" strips of twill tape. Fold each one in half lengthwise.

4 Sandwich each folded strip between the lining and exterior 1" from every side seam. The raw edges should align with the top edges of the lining and exterior; the folded edge of the strips should point down toward the bottom of the hamper. All edges should be flush. Pin the folded strips in place.

5 Sew around the entire perimeter ¼" from the edge. Stop 5" away from the starting point to leave a hole for turning. Turn the lining and exterior right side out by pulling each layer out one at a time and then tucking the lining inside the exterior.

6 Fold the edges of the turning hole in to match the rest of the seam and press with an iron. Also press the twill loops over and into the interior. Edge stitch around the entire top, sewing down the loops and shutting the opening in the process.

7 Stitch each loop's folded edge to the body of the bag through both layers. Stitch right onto the fold at the edge.

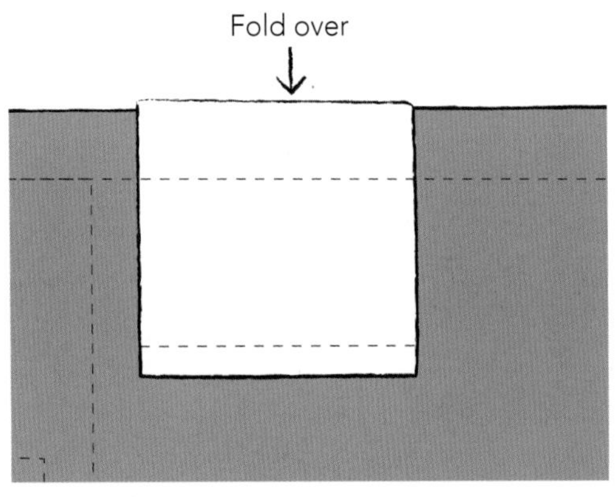

STEPS 6 AND 7

8 Create channels for the long dowels that will slide vertically into the corners of the hampers. Pin the outer and inner side seams together by placing several pins into each seam vertically on the exterior of the hamper. Position the needle ¾" from a vertical seam on the right side of the exterior of the hamper. Beginning at the top hem, stitch straight down the length of the hamper. End ½" from the bottom. Lock stitches in place at the beginning and ending of each seam. Repeat on the left side ¾" from the seam. This creates a 1 ½" channel for each 25" dowel. Give the same treatment to each seam to create four channels.

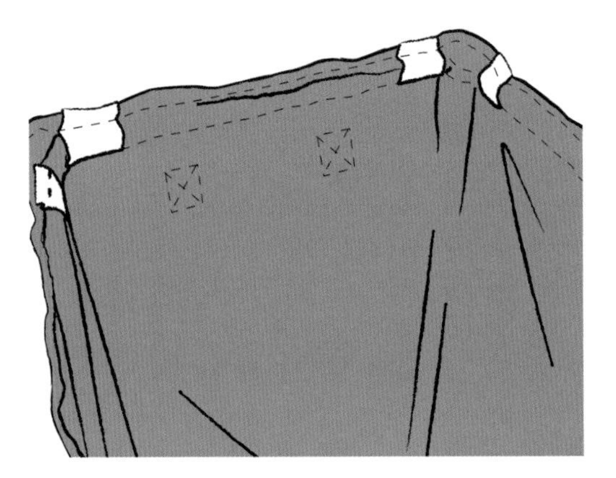

Make the Handles

1 Cut two pieces of exterior fabric measuring 8" × 5". Follow the handle instructions provided in Chapter 1.

2 When the handles are complete, fold each raw end under exactly 1" and press. Center the handles on two sides opposite from one another. Position them 2" below the top edge of the hamper. Lay the handles flat on the outer layer and then scoot each end of the handle ½" closer to the center to make the handle pop out a bit. Sew the handles in place with a boxed X over each 1" fold.

STEP 2

Working with the Dowels

1 Use a hand saw to cut four 25" dowels and four 11" dowels. Use medium coarse sandpaper to sand each end until it's rounded and smooth.

2 Slide a 25" dowel into a vertical channel through the slots in one corner. Arrange the hamper so that the dowel can temporarily slip into the bottom square of the hamper. This enables the dowel to slide all the way through the slot. After the dowel is all the way in, feed the top end back into position so that it fits nicely into the top of the channel. Do this with the remaining three long dowels.

3 Cut a 4" × 62" strip from the interior fabric. Fold each 4" side under ¼" and sew along the edge. Fold the strip in half lengthwise and press. Reopen the strip and fold each side toward the crease. Press. Stitch only along the open side of the long fold.

4 Fasten a safety pin to the end of the cloth tube and feed it through all of the twill loops. One-by-one insert the 11" dowels into the tube and slowly, gently push them through each loop until all four are in and positioned between the long vertical dowels. You will have to do a little adjusting until the fit is just right and each side panel is smooth. When you're done, tie the two ends of the tube in a simple knot.

STEP 4

Make the Cardboard Base

Create a slip cover for the cardboard insert. Fold a 12" × 25" rectangle of the lining fabric in half lengthwise with the right sides facing. Sew up two sides with a ⅛" seam allowance and leave the side opposite of the fold open. Turn the slip cover right side out and insert the piece of cardboard. Fold over the open side twice and press. Stitch closed. Slip the covered cardboard into the bottom of the hamper for more structure and stability. Remove for washing. Set your hamper out for laundry catching!

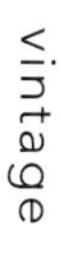

Resources

Supplies

ORGANIC TWILL TAPES

Wayne Mills Co. Inc.: http://www.waynemills.com
NearSea Naturals:
http://www.nearseanaturals.com/
Twill tape used in the Little Forager Skirt:
Pikku Ribbon from http://shop.angelaliguori.com

FABRIC

There are many sources for environmentally friendly fabrics online. I bought hemp for my wedding dress long ago at Harts Fabric and it still remains a great choice for eco fabric. You can find Harts Fabric online at http://www.hartsfabric.com/.

ORGANIC BATTING AND STUFFING

I use NearSea Naturals organic batting from http://www.nearseanaturals.com/.

NOTE: Don't forget to think out of the box: Old flannel sheets and thin towels make wonderful batting.

TEXTILE PAINT AND INK

I prefer Jacquard Textile Colors for freezer printing. Find a large selection at Dharma Trading Co., which you can find online at http://www.dharmatrading.com/.

VersaCraft fabric ink pads work beautifully for nature printing on fabric. Search http://www.etsy.com under supplies with the key words "versacraft fabric ink pad."

FREEZER PAPER

Freezer paper is available at most local grocery stores and at http://www.amazon.com.

TIFFINS

There are many different varieties of this stainless steel lunch container. We love ours from from http://www.to-goware.com/.

Textile History and Details

Levi Strauss has a fascinating section on its website called Heritage at http://www.levistrauss.com/about/heritage.
The British Museum of London offers wonderful photographs of ancient linen at http://www.britishmuseum.org/.
The Organic Trade Association has detailed information about the environmental impact of cotton and wool. Visit http://www.ota.com/index.html.
Find out more about **The Quilts of Gee's Bend** at http://www.quiltsofgeesbend.com/.

Recommended Books

***Reader's Digest Complete Guide to Sewing* by Readers Digest Editors** (Reader's Digest, 8th Edition, 1981, ISBN-10 0895770261 or ISBN-13 9780895770264): Every sewer should have at least one good reference book in her library. This classic is my favorite. The older editions are more comprehensive than the newer ones, so don't hesitate to get a used copy of this classic.

***The Art of Manipulating Fabric* by Colette Wolff** (Chilton Book Company, 1996, ISBN-10 0801984963 or ISBN-13 9780801984969): An extremely thorough guide to incorporating pleats, gathers, ruffles, tucks, and shirring into your sewing projects.

***Printing by Hand: A Modern Guide to Printing with Handmade Stamps, Stencils, and Silk Screens* by Lena Corwin** (STC Craft/A Melanie Falick Book, 2008, ISBN-10 1584796723 or ISBN-13 9781584796725): Straightforward directions for many kinds of printing on various surfaces.

***Print & Stamp Lab: 52 Ideas for Handmade, Upcycled Print Tools* by Traci Bunkers** (Quarry Books, 2010, ISBN-10 1592535984 or ISBN-13 9781592535989): Great ideas that can be incorporated into surface design on recued textiles.

The following are my two favorite books from the 1970s that continue to inspire me today (both have updated and revised editions as they remain classics to many):

***The Illustrated Hassle-Free Make Your Own Clothes Book* by Joan Wiener Bordow and Sharon Rosenberg** (Skyhorse Publishing, 2008, ISBN-10 1602393095 or ISBN-13 9781602393097)

***Living on the Earth* by Alicia Bay Laurel** (Villard, 2000, ISBN-10 1586853430)

Stencils and Templates

Arithmetic Pillows

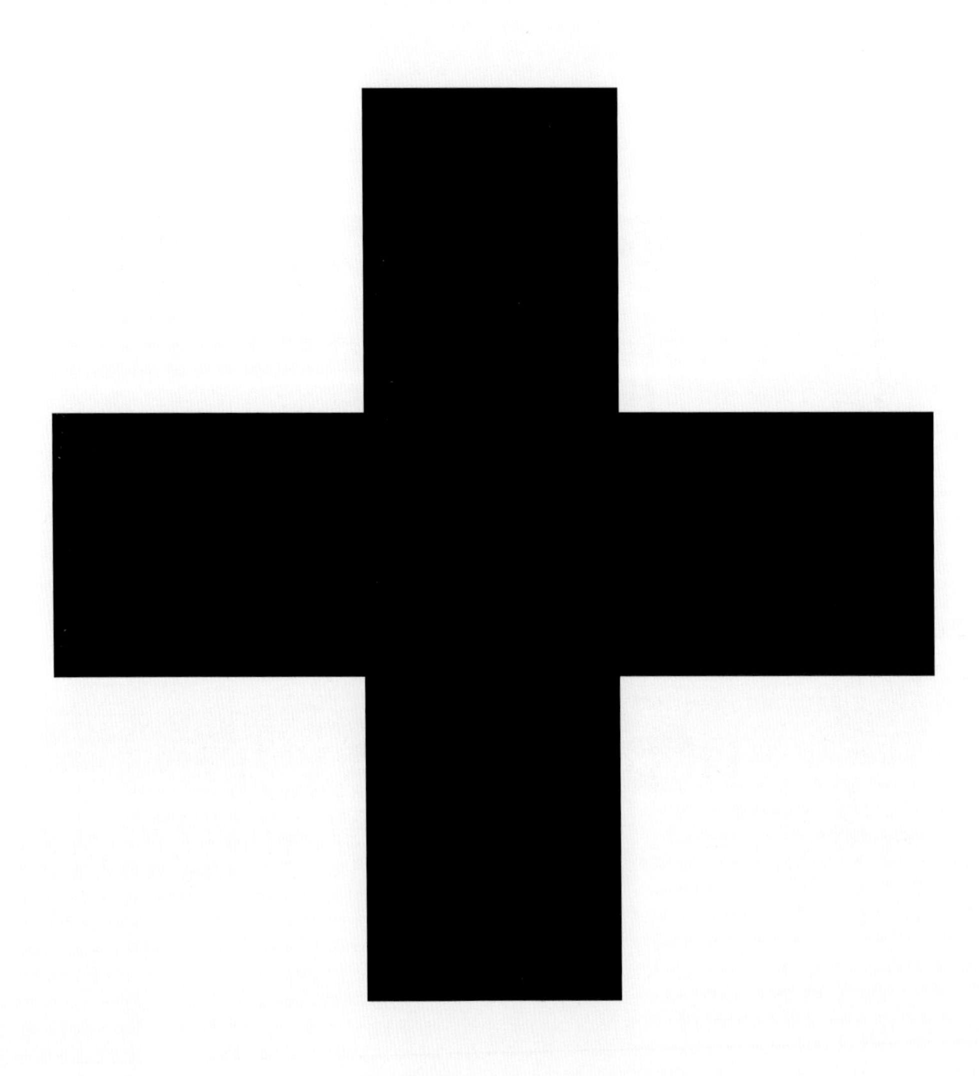

Portfolio
Reversible Summer Sling

Onion and Garlic Sacks

Inspiration Board

Pillow Pal

NOTE: ENLARGE BY 2%
FINAL SIZE SHOULD BE APPROX 8½" × 11"

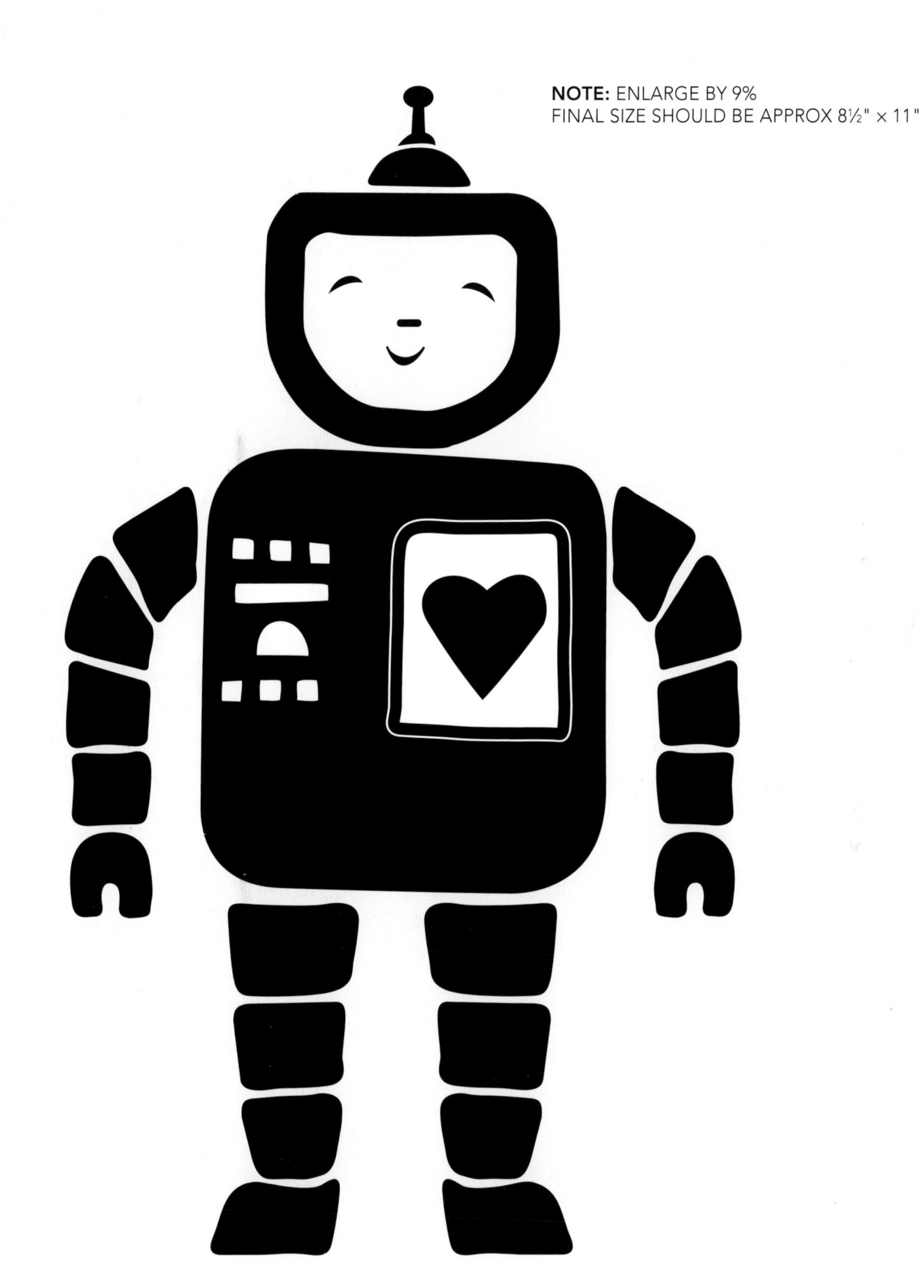

NOTE: ENLARGE BY 9%
FINAL SIZE SHOULD BE APPROX 8½" × 11"

Little Forager Skirt

Insulated Lunch Sack

Barn Throw

Double Duty Oven Mitt

350°

400°

Luggage Tags

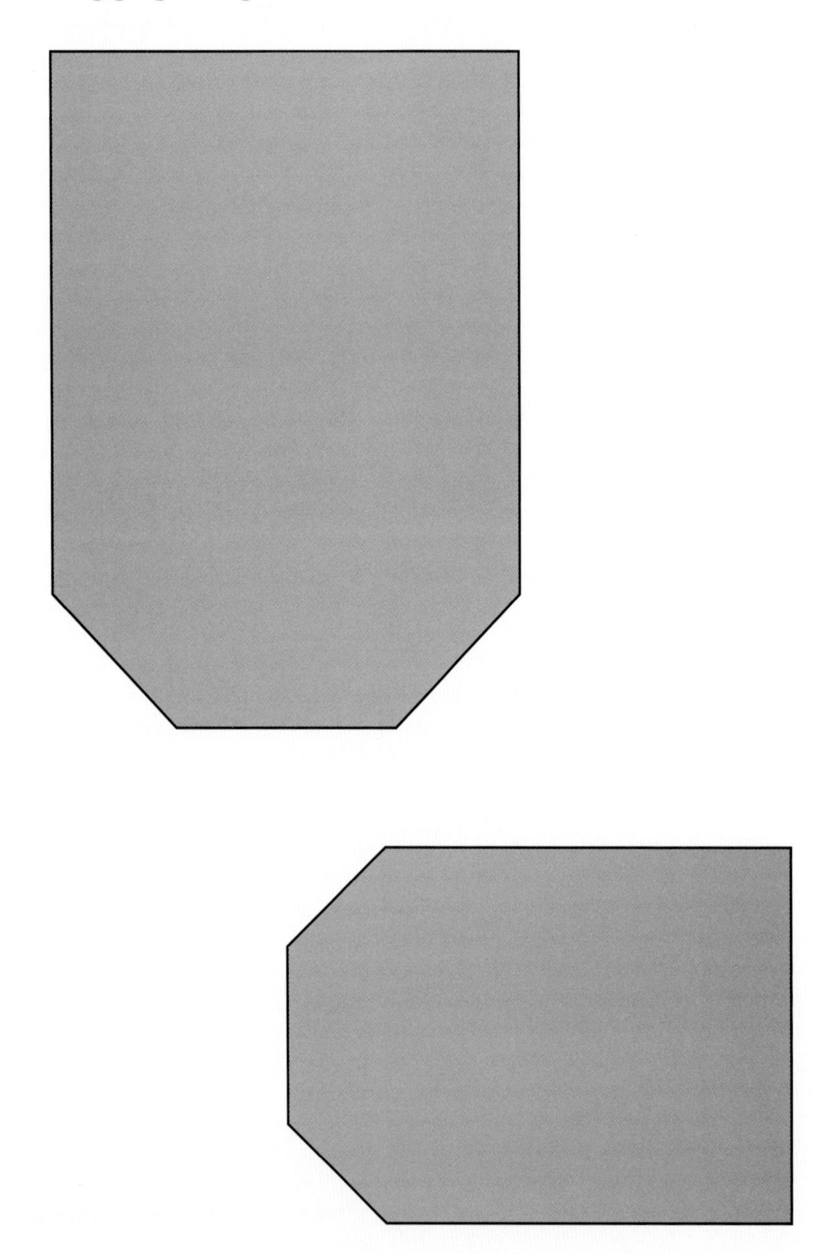

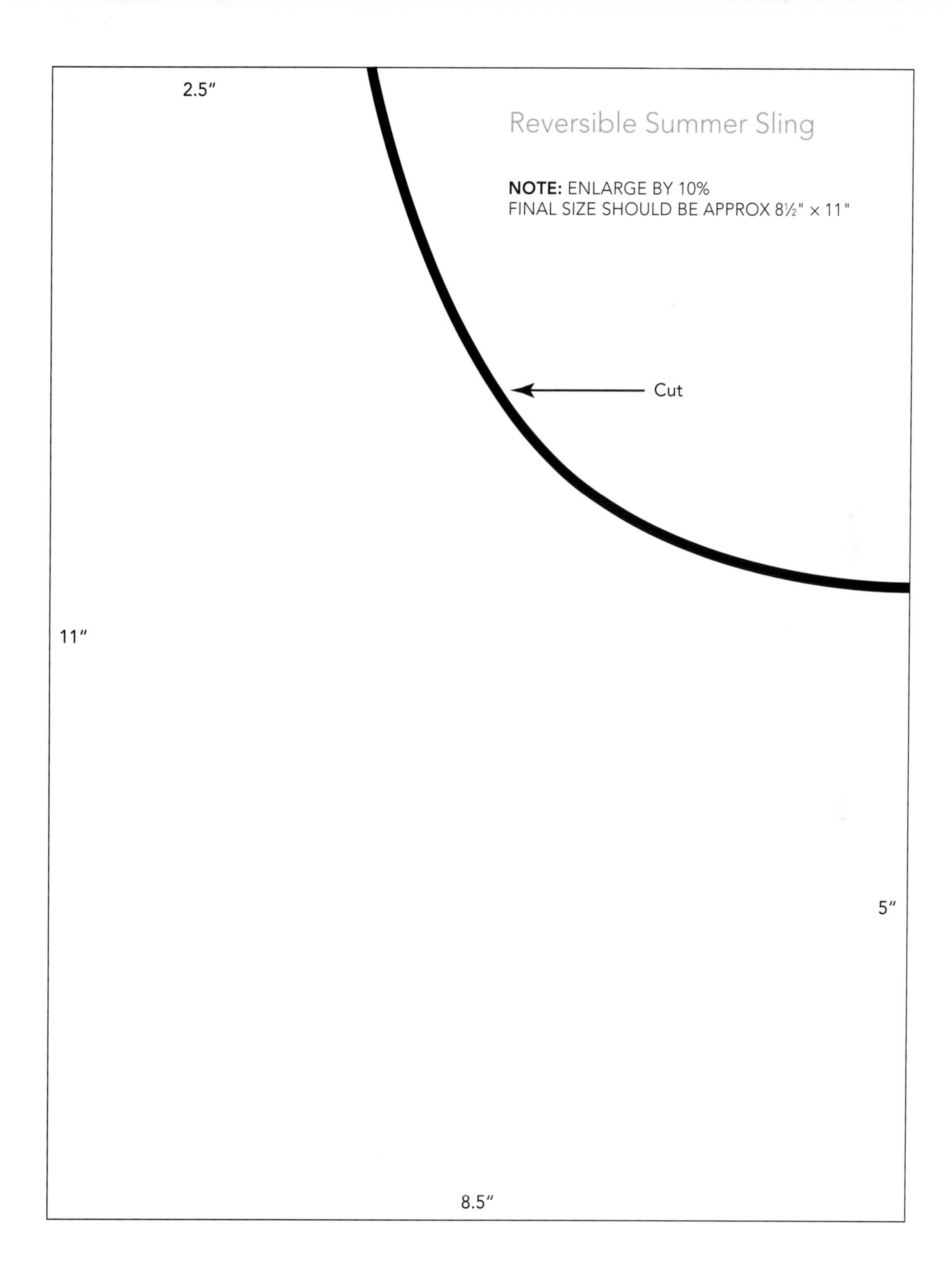
2.5″
Reversible Summer Sling
NOTE: ENLARGE BY 10%
FINAL SIZE SHOULD BE APPROX 8½" × 11"
Cut
11″
5″
8.5″

About the Author

Maya Donenfeld's distinct designs utilize sustainable resources and fibers while weaving in elements from the natural world. She finds the imperfection of handmade endlessly inspiring and seeks out simple, and often humble, materials to transform into useful items of beauty. She is passionate about encouraging others to find their unique creative voice and gain confidence in their own capable hands. Her award-winning website is filled with projects, inspiration, and eco tutorials to light a fire under anyone wanting to artfully recycle, repurpose, and reinvent.

Maya has contributed to many books, and her work has been featured in these magazines: *Country Living*, all first four issues of *Green Craft Magazine, Sew Hip, Where Women Create, Family Circle, Artful Blogging, Food Network Magazine*, and *Create With Me.*

Maya lives with her husband and two children down a country road, in an old farmhouse in the Fingerlakes region of New York.

Index